Cautious Aggression:
Defending Modern Football

Defensive schemes to combat spread offenses.

Cody Alexander

Copyright © 2017 Cody Alexander & MatchQuarters.com

All rights reserved.

ISBN: 1548099732
ISBN-13: 978-1548099732

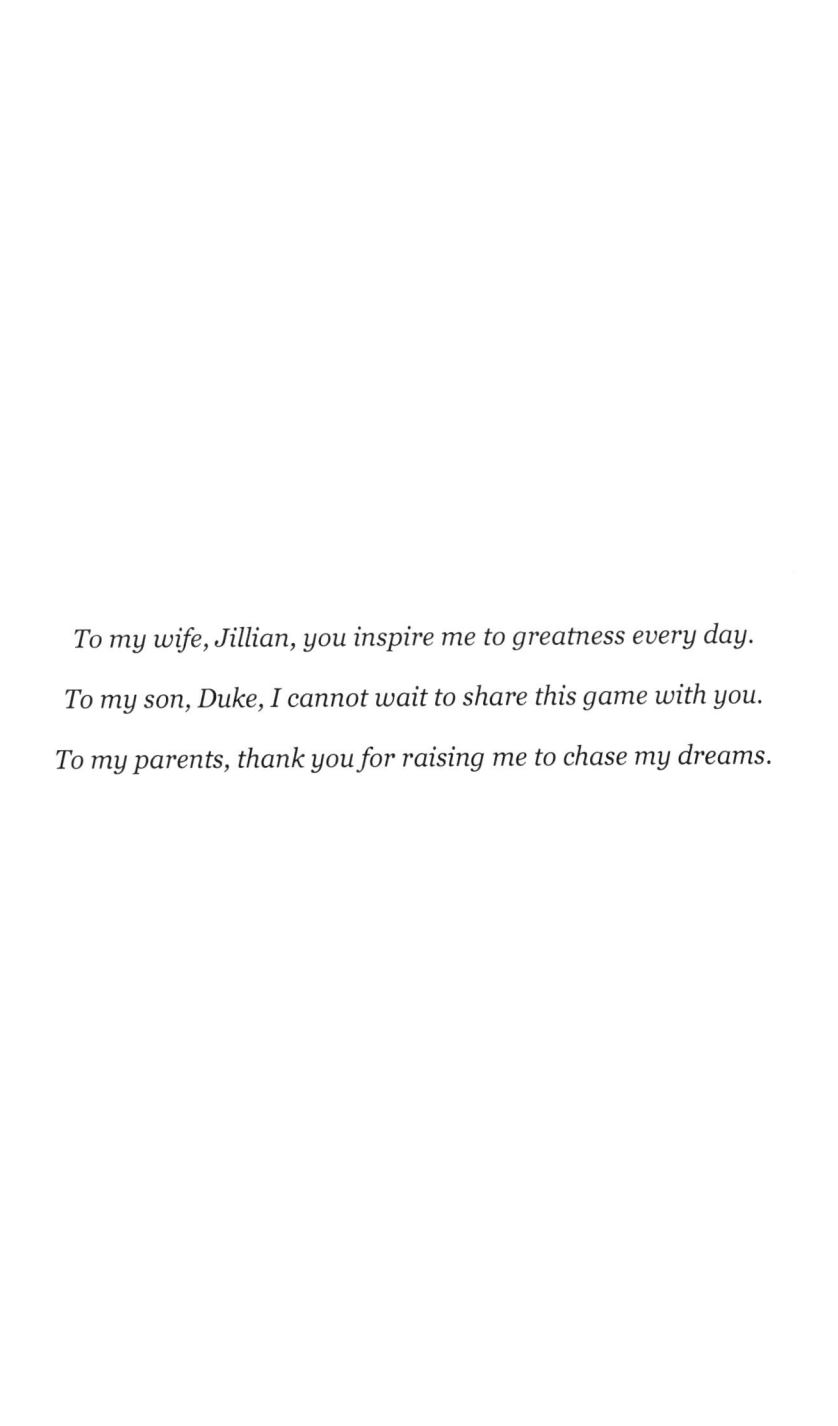

To my wife, Jillian, you inspire me to greatness every day.

To my son, Duke, I cannot wait to share this game with you.

To my parents, thank you for raising me to chase my dreams.

CONTENTS

	Acknowledgments	i
	Prologue :: Falling Forward	1

The Why

1	The Argument for Two-High	23
2	Defending the Modern Spread Offense	33
3	Defending Run/Pass Options	41
4	Systematic Creativity of a Quarters Defense	55
5	The Art of Match Quarters	73

The How

6	All About the Cover Down	83
7	Designing a Modern Defense	99
8	Setting the Strength	107
9	Defending Formations into the Boundary	115
10	Defending Motion	133
	Conclusion	149
	Thank You	155

ACKNOWLEDGMENTS

This book is a collection of thoughts derived from three years of defending the greatest offense ever to be assembled and my time within the high school ranks. During my time at Baylor, Art Briles and Phillip Montgomery were able to create an offensive juggernaut that tested the traditional theories of defense. During the 2013 season in particular, we would start the season scoring over 50 points in five of our first six games, only being held to 35 by Kansas State (who runs a version of the defense described in this book). Working daily against an offense like that challenges your beliefs about defensive football to the core.

Phil Bennett did the impossible at Baylor. He took a defense that was at the bottom of Division I football, and in three years made it one of the best defenses in the country. The schemes and ideas in this book are a direct reflection of the thought process the defensive staff at Baylor used to defend some of the best offenses in the country from 2011 to 2016.

The Big XII is no joke when it comes to offensive football. This is a conference that boasts some of the greatest offensive minds in the county. Working daily against one of the best ever in Art Briles refined the theories on defending the spread that you see in this book. No defense is perfect, but the defensive schemes described in this book work and can be implemented at any level of football.

Coaching at the lower levels of football bring its own issues to the table that many Division I football teams do not face. *Cautious Aggression: Defending Modern Football* is written for all coaches. The experiences I gained at Baylor combined with my experiences at the high school level have given me a unique perspective on defensive football. Many of the concepts and theories in this book have been adjusted to fit the needs of high school and small college coaches around the country.

As the spread becomes more of the norm in all regions of this country it is important for coaches everywhere to have a resource for defending the spread. *Cautious Aggression: Defending Modern Football* is that resource for coaches. The schemes described in this book are tried and true methods for defending some of the best offenses this country has seen. Come learn "The Art of X."

- Cody Alexander, MatchQuarters.com

Prologue :: Falling Forward

"If I'm going to fall, I don't want to fall back on anything, except my faith. I want to fall... forward. At least I figure that way I'll see what I'm about to hit. ...Fall forward." – Denzel Washington

--

This book does not exist without Phil Bennett, Jim Gush and Colin Shillinglaw. All three opened their arms to me when I stepped on Baylor's campus in 2011. Without their kindness and generosity I would not be here today, writing this book. Colin, or "Shaq" as he was known in the office, got my foot in the door at Baylor, Bennett imprinted his vast football knowledge on a young and hungry coach, and Gush kept me sane as I was literally put to a baptism by fire. My three years at Baylor are some of the toughest years of my life. Not only was I a graduate assistant, but I got married and had a child within the first year I was there. Needless to say, I needed all the help I could get on and off the field. These three men are a vital part of my story and I am still close to Bennett and Gush today.

I didn't play Division I football or I have a "famous"

coaching dad. I got to Baylor because I refused to except that an outsider like me couldn't get a graduate assistant position at a Power Five program. Bennett and Gush, not only nurtured my love for the game of football, but in many cases taught me how to be a man and a professional. They ignored the fact that I was a "nobody" and pushed me to my limits to see what I could do. Though this book is dedicated to my wife and son, I feel it is my duty to explain my journey.

--

To get my foot in the door at Baylor I had struck a deal with then Director of Football Operations, Colin Shillinglaw. I would help him with the day-to-day operations while I attended graduate school and he would get me in front of the coaches (though he did encourage me to start with the defensive side, Briles keeps the offense in the "family"). Shillinglaw was the only DFO that answered my calls when I was attempting to make the leap from the high school ranks. At the time my future wife and I were living in Waxahachie, Texas, a small town near south Dallas. I called every college in the metroplex: North Texas, SMU, and TCU. No one answered except SMU. They gave me the "We'll put your resume on file," spiel. I would not be deterred.

My dream has always been to be a college coach, and after two years of coaching in the high school ranks I was going to put in all my chips. After graduating from Southern Nazarene University in May of 2009, I took my first coaching job at Deer Creek HS in Edmond, Oklahoma. Luck would have it that while I was student teaching at the middle school, not only was the teacher I was working under moving on to be a principal, but the football team needed a secondary coach. I jumped at the opportunity. My wife was still finishing up here degree at SNU, so it was a perfect fit. Even though I was only there for a year, I learned a great deal form the men that I coached with. The head coach at the time, Grant Gower (current Offensive Coordinator at Oklahoma Baptist), is a man of integrity and gave me my first opportunity at coaching varsity football.

I am notoriously over ambitious. John Lang (former Defensive Coordinator) and Will Wortmann (former Assistant Head Coach/Offensive Line) helped me to keep my mind right and my ego in check. Both of them are tremendous men and I cannot express enough gratitude for mentoring me, even if just for a year. I still communicate with several of the people and players I met during my brief time at DC. It is a fantastic community and school district, but with the completion of my wife's degree we looked to move closer to her family and into football country, Texas.

    The 2010 season was my toughest by far. Andy Chester, the Athletic Director for LifeSchools, gave me an opportunity that many of the coaches I contacted would not, a varsity position on the football staff. Texas is a proud football state and being young with little experience is not an easy road to travel, particularly when looking for a varsity assistant position.

    LifeSchool Waxahachie was entering their first year as a varsity football team. Being the overly ambitious and energetic coach I was, I decided to jump at the opportunity instead of waiting my turn somewhere else. I'm glad I did. Life Waxahachie is where I learned to lose, never give up, and solidified my desire for something more, in my case coaching Division I football. We did not win a game that year, but the players and coaches never gave up. The average score for that season was 6-56. Yes, that is correct; your eyes are not lying to you. As a defensive coach it was a very humbling experience, but Life Waxahachie gave me so much more.

    I was part of the program's first victory, a win over Scurry-Rosser's Junior Varsity. It was awesome. You would have thought our kids had won the Super Bowl, and I felt that way too. Many coaches would have scoffed at the idea of coaching at a small (2A at the time) charter school in south Dallas, but it was such a rewarding experience. To see young players never give up, even when we all knew we were going to lose, is something that can recharge your battery. As a coach I got to learn first-hand how to manage a team, motivate players, and build confidence in the face of defeat. I always smile when I pass the sparkling new campus in Waxahachie. I still communicate with many of the coaches I worked with (there were only four of us!).

Mark Larson (currently coaching in Missouri) is a brave man and took a job most coaches would not. He inspired me to be the young ambitious coach that I am today. Michael Hirtzel, and his relaxed attitude, really helped me get through the season. I am notably high-strung and "Type A," most defensive coaches are. Hirtzel is the typical laid-back offensive coach. I needed that. He allowed me to smile and take deep breaths. Lastly, Wade McKee (currently still at Life Waxahachie) was my brother in arms. We spent most of the time trying to keep each other sane. Wade is a worker. He definitely taught me the value of a work ethic and the drive to get better than you were the day before.

Like I stated earlier, my experience at Life Waxahachie challenged me to take the next step in my career. If these players and coaches were going to refuse to lose in the face of adversity, then how could I accept anything less from myself? With the coaxing of my wife and my family I decided to do the unthinkable, kick down the doors of Division I football. I would not accept anything other than an answer of Y-E-S.

--

People always ask me how I was able to obtain a graduate assistant position at Baylor, especially under Briles who is notoriously a close to the vest coach. I got my opportunity because I refused to take no for an answer and luck happened to be on my side.

In the spring of 2011 I had come to a crossroads in my coaching career. I loved football, but I was not satisfied with where I was or the coach I was becoming. I wanted more; responsibility, knowledge, and professionalism. I wanted an upgrade. The question was how to do it? While at Deer Creek I was able to meet some coaches that had ties to colleges, but nothing really worked out. I finished my playing career at SNU in 2008, but there were no prospects of staying on there or moving on to another college, which is why I jumped at the chance to coach at Deer Creek.

My dream since I was a youth was to be a college coach, and two years into my career I didn't want to wait any longer on making that dream a reality. I figured the only way I could force my way in was to literally force my way in, so I took the GRE and called programs.

The plan was simple; if I could get into grad school then I would park myself at the football facility and give the staff no choice. Remember, I am overly ambitious. As I stated, no one picked up the phone around Dallas. My wife's sister was attending Baylor at the time and I had fallen in love with the campus and the school the few times we went to visit. At the time, Baylor was scraping the bottom of the Big 12 and I felt it would be a great place to get my start. Who wanted to work there anyway, right? I attacked the GRE with vigor and was blessed to receive a great score. I applied and was accepted into Baylor's Sports Management Master's program. I had nothing to lose.

By the grace of God, Shill picked up the phone. I explained to him I was going to be getting my master's from Baylor and would be there in the summer. I would do whatever it took to be part of the program. Luckily, Shill needed as much help as he could get (Briles never kept a large off-field staff – bare minimum). I was elated and had no idea how the next three years would change my life.

--

I will never forget the first time I "officially" met Phil

Bennett. It was the summer of 2011 and I had already been at Baylor for several weeks. Camp season was in full swing and I was diving head first into my master's program, working part-time for the Education Department, and trying to get my foot in the door. At that time, Baylor was not Baylor and Robert Griffin III had not won the Heisman... yet. Things were about to get interesting in 2011.

My desk was located in the Graduate Assistant's office, parked right next to the door. It was a tiny room located opposite of Shill's office and really the only place I was allowed to be. My desk faced out the door, so I saw Coach Bennett walk by several times a day, but I decided it was best to let him come to me. I offered my assistance to him once I get to Baylor, but I didn't press the issue. I figured I would work my way into being noticed. I am a coach's son and learned early on to keep my mouth shut and work. I went back to my fundamentals.

There are no guarantees in football. Your career trajectory really boils down to who you know and circumstance. I arrived at Baylor at the perfect time. Bennett had just got the defensive coordinator position that spring and needed as much help as he could get. He had brought his own intern, but I figured I could find a way to help.

My nose was always in a book because I knew there was no guarantee that I would get a shot and I wasn't going to leave without my master's. Bennett would walk by me several times a day and see me propped up behind my desk reading a book. If you know Bennett, then you know that his mind works in a much different way than most. He's inquisitive and truly a genius. That being said he is also crass and blunt. The GA that I worked with at the time, Adrian Haywood, coined the term "Emotional Terrorist."

"Who the f*** are you?" asked Bennett, slight smirk on his face. Startled, I dropped my book and almost fell backwards out of my chair. If you know Bennett, than you know he has a tendency to jolt you the first time you meet him. His independent spirit and uncompromising resiliency is something that I have always admired about Coach. From the start Bennett never promised me anything other than I could have a chair in the room. That was all I needed.

--

He began to describe that he always sees me reading and wanted to know who I was because I'm here all the time. I explained to him that I was getting my master's and I wanted to coach college football, so I enrolled and started volunteering. Bennett nodded his head and stated, "I already got an intern," turned and walked back to his office. I stared at the door frame for what felt like a whole minute. I was speechless, which was a new feeling for me. One thing I am not is a quitter, and I wasn't going to let the fact that he had already brought an intern with him deter me. Needing to do something, I dropped my book and hurried down the hall after him. It is only a couple steps from the GA office to Bennett's desk, so I needed to think quickly what I was going to say and gain some composure. First impressions are everything.

--

Later I would find out that Bennett confronted Shill about "hiring" me to help him (which was not the case). I hadn't been there more than a week and had already created drama. My future wasn't looking bright. I quickly had to explain my plan to Bennett. Luckily he accepted my plan and would allow me to sit in meetings. Soon after, work was being thrown my way and I was grinding to get it done.

It was challenging and hard, but I loved every minute of it. Those first six months on the job are some of my favorite memories of coaching. By the time the season rolled around I was in charge of the recruiting board and gaining traction on becoming the leader of our opponent scout. By the time we played Texas A&M I was placed in charge of the scout team. I was well on my way to earning the trust of the defensive staff.

Bennett's mentorship has been invaluable. He challenged me every day to be the best and then do better the next day. He taught me to be a professional and exposed my weaknesses as a coach. His brutal honesty was exactly what I needed at that point in my life. I had become jaded and disillusioned with the game. He gave me back my love for football and for that I am truly grateful. He taught me to have attention to detail and analyze everything and while doing so, have fun. We worked hard at Baylor, but I was home every night. Bennett is not easy to work for, and he will be the first to tell you that, but as tough as his exterior was he loved me and embraced me. The schemes that are in this book are a derivative of his thought process and my version of how to defend the modern spread.

--

Though my initial goal of becoming a full-time Division 1 football coach failed, the knowledge I attained while at Baylor was well worth the failure. For about a year after I was done at Baylor I resented the fact that I failed. As I get further away from my time there I have realized that titles and positions come and go, but it is the relationships that you establish that are truly meaningful. That staff was one of the closest knit staffs I have been around.

No one was leaving after the 2013 season, which was surprising because Baylor had won its first Big 12 championship. As a young GA that isn't good for business. There is no playbook for becoming a full-time Division I coach. The path is different for everyone. Some coaches rise like rockets to the top while others live in the black hole that is Quality Control for much of their career, like a 30-something minor leaguer. Just trying to hold on for one more season, one more coaching change. Looking back, it is disgusting to think that you are rooting for other men to get fired. They have families too. Who am I to say I'm better, or I deserve a shot?

As I stated, no one left and the connections I did have were not looking for a fresh faced GA. Modern college football is rigged differently than in the past. It used to be you paid your dues as a GA and then moved on when your time was up or a coach left. No ADs have to answer to boosters, fans, and corporations. Many coaches feel they can't take chances when hiring guys. I have always felt, if I am looking for a doctor I want someone who has learned from the best and has cutting edge innovations at their disposal. That is not what always happens.

Many times ADs and coaches have to turn to retread coaches who have "experience." That is why many times young coaches have to GA at two different places, waiting for their call-up. Some even go the Quality Control route, making little to no money. For me, that wasn't the life I wanted for my family. Say what you want, but the older I get I am more about quality of life than a title.

Leaving Baylor "empty handed" was devastating to my ego. I had given so much to that university and we had tremendous success while I was there. It took me several years to get over it. Failure is part of life. It is a constant. The more we fight with it, the worse it gets. One of my favorite quotes deals with failure and the pressure the modern coach feels to be successful:

"If you find yourself in a hole, stop digging." – Will Rogers
Feeling sorry for my self was not going to make things better.

--

I had completed my degree several weeks before the Fiesta Bowl and was trying as hard as I could to land a job. I had been offered several off-field positions, but none of them paid well enough for me to bring my family along. My son, Duke, was born after my second year at Baylor. He wasn't even one when we flew to Phoenix for the Fiesta Bowl. What a time to be alive!

Football is a tough sport, especially on family members of coaches. I didn't feel comfortable sacrificing my wife and one year old son's wellbeing to chase a $30,000 job that would move my family across country. I couldn't look them in the eye while they suffered. I'll never forget one coach selling me on a job by explaining that his offensive coordinator's family didn't even live with him, instead choosing to reside in Las Vegas. He noted that a lot of coaches do this. To me, that wasn't logical. I'm going to move across the country for a $30,000 job and I am supposed to fly my family back and forth (and just video chat every day)? I didn't want to watch my son grow up on a tablet screen.

--

To be honest, there are some people that will read this and say I am dumb for not taking the job. I have wrestled with this many times over the past year. The "what ifs" and "what could have been," all swirled in my head for the next year. At the end of the day we all have to make decisions. As Ryan Holiday put it in his book *Ego is the Enemy*:

"*To be or to do – life is a constant roll call.*"

In this section of the book, Holiday explains that in life we have to make choices. That there is an unavoidable fork in the road. We can either *be* somebody or *do* something. To be somebody is what our culture has impressed upon us from a young age. The problem with being somebody is that we have to make compromises and many times those compromises make us lose ourselves. We make choices selfishly and don't realize the damage we are doing to those that love us, our family. Yes, you may get that job you covet or the title you are looking for, but you have lost the foundation of who you are. Look around the coaching world. There are a lot of coaches that are divorced, have alienated their family and kids, but for what? A well-paying job? A championship? Those are things that can never give back to you. They are just, things. Don't ever lose sight of the fact that football is a game; a team game at that.

The other choice a person can make is to do something. Marcus Aurelius once stated, *"Waste no more time arguing about what a good man should be. Be one."* What Aurelius is saying is quit trying to be and just do! Do what is right and the recognition will come, or maybe it won't, but at the end of the day you can lay your head down knowing you did the best you could. You have your family intact, your players love you, and you are doing something with your life.

This question haunted me when I read Holiday's book last summer. Was I trying to be someone all while sacrificing what it really took to accomplish the goals I wanted to achieve? We all at some point have to face the inner demon that is ego. For me, it came in November of 2015. Until then I was trying to be somebody, but I wasn't doing what I needed to do in order to keep my family intact and my life.

--

I made one of the hardest decisions of my life in February 2014. I decided to go back to coaching high school football and wait my turn to be called back up. It has now been three seasons since I worked at Baylor, and going on four. The lessons I learned while at Baylor have carried me through a lot of learning experiences since leaving that February. Sometimes, what seems to be a curse, turns into blessings that you could not fathom while you were blinded by circumstance.

The doors that were opened for me at Baylor continue to open doors today. It is amazing looking back on my journey and how extremely lucky I was to even step foot into Baylor's football facility. I had absolutely no idea what was in store for me and the whirlwind that would be the next three years. From RGIII and the Heisman, to a Big 12 championship and devastating loss to UCF in the Fiesta Bowl, and the reality that I was not going to be a full-time Division I coach.

My journey to where I am today has tremendous highs as well as devastating lows, but the knowledge that was given to me by Phil Bennett and Art Briles will live with me forever. Coaching

Division I football is not for everybody, and it is not easy. It is a grind that cannot be described unless you have been there. I not only got my master's in Sports Management from Baylor, but I got a doctorate in defending the spread.

Bennett is a legend in his own right and one of the most respected defensive minds in football. Say what you want about Briles as a man, but his legacy as an offensive mind cannot be questioned. In my opinion Briles and Phillip Montgomery (current head coach at Tulsa) created one of the greatest offenses of all time (and I got to defend it every day!). The knowledge I received while at Baylor is timeless. I got to learn firsthand how to deal with the extremes of the spread offense from the best minds in football. I absorbed everything I could about defensive football and how to counteract the modern spread. Detailed in this book are my thoughts on defending modern football.

Cody Alexander

--

"Fortune doesn't have the long reach we suppose, she can only lay siege to those who hold her tight. So let's step back from her as much as possible." – Seneca, *Moral Letters*

--

When defending the spread a defensive coordinator can choose two paths. One, is the offensive route of infinite blitzes and exhausting movements. Or two, a strategy of flexibility and adaptiveness, or as I like to call it *cautious aggression*. The schemes detailed in this book are of the latter. Defensive football is reactionary. Be overly aggressive and the spread kills you quickly. Better to stay even, keep everything in front, and adapt. In football terms, "Bend and don't break."

Cody Alexander

The Why

Cody Alexander

The Argument for Two-High

"The cautious seldom err." – Confucius

--

Match quarters and other derivatives of the two-high scheme are not passive in nature. Rather, the schemes themselves mesh with the reactionary nature of defensive football. Staying balanced and adaptive, flexible and structured, these are keys to victory.

--

The base alignments used in any defense should be sufficient, and sound enough to carry a team through any game. Defensive coordinators that feel they have to "run something" tend to panic and call the wrong play, or blitz into a situation that calls for them to be passive. A defense's best first down call should be its base. Against modern spread teams, spinning to single-high or blitzing off the edge every down will get a team beat. There are times in a game that a defensive coordinator must pressure an offense, but not on every play.

Simply put, defense is about adjustments. A team's base

should be able to align against any formation that the offense chooses to set up. The rules set within the base allow quick and easy alignments. A defense should not be able to "Omaha" or "Kill" their base defense. If this is the case, then a defensive coordinator should change the base alignments or scrap the defense. There is nothing more important than being able to line up correctly and execute a base defense. This starts at the foundations of defensive design. When developing a base defense it is important to formulate how the defense will line up against every possible set (2x2, 3x1, 3x2, 2x1, etc.). Once formulated, the base alignments should be gap sound and plus one in pass distribution and run fits. Having a plus one mentality is possible, and the best way to achieve this is through a split field coverage quarters scheme, or a two-high safety look.

    Coaches that argue against a two-high look tend to make the argument that you cannot stay in the same place all the time or the offense will carve the defense up. By spinning, they argue, a defense can disguise and confuse the quarterback and offensive coordinator. Playing a static defense will get you beat, but quarters coverage is not static, it is flexible. Teams that spin a majority of the time actually create more one-on-one opportunities for the offense. Ask any offensive coordinator and they will tell you they want one-on-one matchups. For the offense it comes down to picking the best matchup and attacking it. Spinning to single-high also puts pressure on a defense's corners. Whether Cover 1 or Cover 3, the corners tend to be forced into man situations and the defense is vulnerable to higher percentage throws.

A quarters look creates a balanced defensive set, does not lose leverage points, and forces the offense to work harder. There is a reason many defensive coordinators quickly went away from the "Split 44" version of the 4-2-5 as the spread became the norm across the country. With the growing popularity of the spread, the vertical pressure created by multi-receiver formations and the width of these formations was too much for many single-high defenses. Cover 3 defenses struggle with defending the seam (vertical hash routes) because the overhangs must react and push with any underneath route. This conflict lends itself to high percentage throws by the offense. The closer the route gets to the quarterback, the higher the completion rate. Routes such as slants, hitches, and simple seam routes are combined with other routes to force the seam defender to react. With only one safety in the middle of the field, all the quarterback has to do is look him off.

Versus the run, by rolling a safety in a certain direction a defense is largely losing a box player, which ironically is what spinning is supposed to do, add to the box. Whether it is a 2x2 set or 3x1 set, the player that is dropping down is moving closer to the line of scrimmage, and the defense is taking away a potential box player from somewhere else. In a two-high safety look, a defense can stay balanced and the away side safety can help with any cutback, even inserting himself into the box if need be. If rolled up, it is hard for that player to help with cutback because of angles. See the image below:

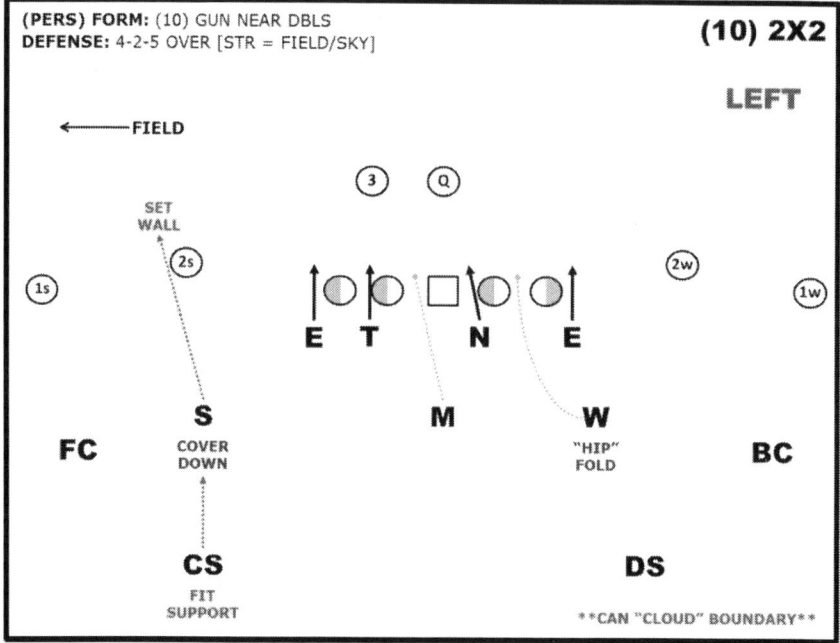

A two-high look allows a defense to have a nine-man box and two or four deep in the pass. The most efficient defenses force the offense to do things they do not want to do. They make offenses change. Against spread teams, spinning to single-high gives the offense space to the outside, and an easy seam throw in play-action. When teams throw the ball, they want completions. Teams take shots down the field and some more than others do, but it is the defense's job to make the offense work for those shots. Playing a two-high scheme compresses the field and forces the offense to throw outside (low completion throws).

Defenses that press the corners within their quarters scheme, force the offense to change even more. When a defense presses the corners they are eliminating route choices. Most offenses when faced with a team that presses try to throw vertical routes or slants. Eliminating route choices makes the offense predictable. Defense is reactionary, it is important to create a defense that can adjust to anything an offense throws at it while also forcing it to change at the same time.

The design of press quarters relies on the law of averages. Any offensive coach will admit when a receiver is pressed it eliminates the route choices. To a defensive coach, being able to eliminate play calls from an opposing offense is money in the bank. There is a run fit piece to the design too. The linebackers in Michigan State's press quarters defense are ultra-aggressive in the run game. By eliminating the outside receivers, the defense has literally shrunk the field. The shrunken field allows the linebackers to be aggressive. The safeties align over the slot receivers and act as stopgaps in case of pass. The safeties' eyes focus on the slot receivers, while the linebackers focus on the end man on the line of scrimmage and react to the low-hat (run) or high-hat (pass) read given. This aggressiveness allows the defense to have a seven-man box just on alignment. The secondary, because it is quarters coverage (Four Read), plays the offensive set much like man and matching the routes. See the diagram below:

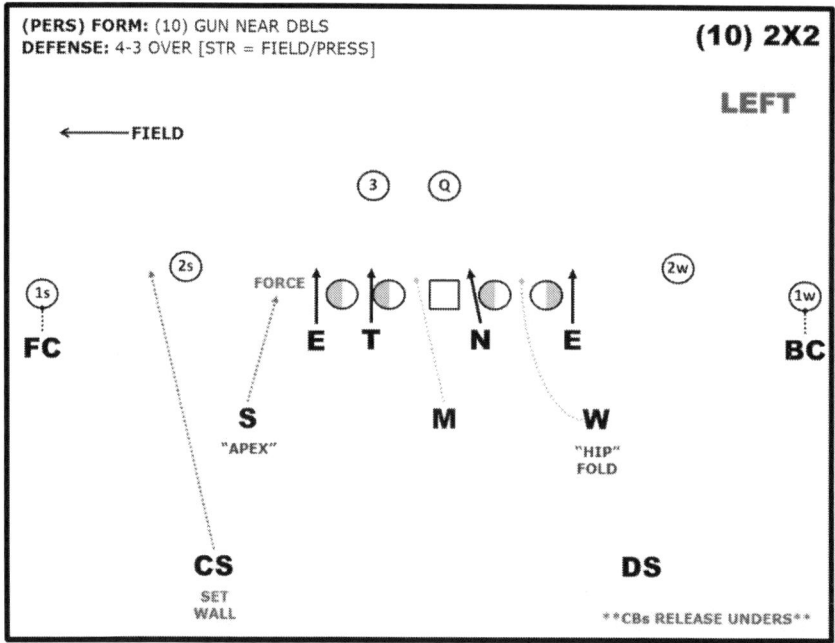

Some coaches will argue that pressing an outside receiver is dangerous and leaves you vulnerable to the quick outside throw (fade in particular). This is true if you play a hard press corner. The hard corner technique, seen in a Tampa 2 defense, stresses strong, physical play underneath, and utilizes safeties with range to combat the outside fade by the #1 receiver. The problem with Tampa 2 is the defense's Mike linebacker is always in a run/pass conflict because he must cover the middle third of the defense yet also stuff the run as a primary box fitter. As college teams have shifted to utilizing quarters schemes, the need for large physical corners has gone to the wayside. Teams that defend the spread on a daily basis need fast, fluid corners that can run and match up with speedy receivers (this goes for the safeties too).

--

In match quarters, the defense is running a pseudo-man scheme where the back four are either playing man (corners) or bracket concepts (linebackers under/safeties over). The next evolution for quarters schemes came in the form of soft press by the corners on the outside receivers. This is not the old school, in your face "hard" press; this is more like a point guard in basketball press. By backing the corners up to a depth of 1.5 to 2 yards, the corner has taken away the chance of error by being too physical. The depth allows the corners to feather off (hot-foot shuffle) and makes the receiver choose which stem point to attack. Once the receiver has made their move, it is easy for the corner to react, of-hand jam, and get to cut-off (fade) or "top" the route (slant). Soft press allows the corner the freedom to react instead of guessing. The press alignment also eliminates certain routes from the route tree. By pressing, the averages suggest a corner will face a deep route (fade/post) or a slant. Aligning inside, the corner can drive on the slant, wall off a post, or force the receiver to the sideline on a fade (forcing the lowest percentage throw).

When utilizing a soft press technique, a defense can eliminate routes and attack the outside receiver. By shrinking the field, the safeties and linebackers are able to compress the line of scrimmage and shrink their focus of play. This type of match quarters acts as a bracket defense for the slot receivers and frees up the linebackers to be aggressive and downhill on the run.

Safeties in a press quarters scheme do not change responsibility from regular quarters. They are still under any deep route by the #1 receiver coming into the field (intermediate zone), and can react quicker versus run/pass option (RPO) screens (bubble/switches). In terms of teaching soft press, most players have played basketball at some point in their life. It is easy to relate the soft press technique back to the basketball court. In basketball, a defender is discouraged from making physical contact. The soft press technique may take the physicality out of the press, but it allows the corner the freedom to react instead of guess. The corner is forcing the receiver to show his cards, then reacting with an off-hand jam working to the cut-off (fade) or to "top" the route (slant). A two-high safety scheme combined with pressed corners forces the offense into low percentage throws or "shots."

Deep shots are the equivalent of a three-point shot in basketball. Like Golden State in the NBA, some teams have developed their whole offense around them (see Baylor, Oklahoma State or the whole Big 12 in fact). The point of split field quarters is to make the deep ball harder to complete for the offense, while also forcing them to throw it. By aligning in a two-high scheme, a defense can bracket the easiest throws to the slot (middle of the field/seam).

Offensive coaches want to look for the one-on-one matchups. Spinning to single-high creates matchup issues for the defense because at least one linebacker must cover the slot (less accomplished cover man vs. potentially the offense's best receiver). As the modern spread offense developed, many teams began to put their best receivers inside at slot because of the physical mismatch and single coverage. As defenses spin to stop the run, they are creating one-on-one matchups with the offense's best receivers. Spinning to single-high versus a 3x1 set pressures the Sam linebacker in pass coverage, and weakens the defense to the boundary. Offenses know they have a one-on-one with the Sam and backside corner if a defense chooses to spin.

A two-high safety team forces the "shot" teams to throw outside for low percentage throws. In the high school ranks, and even in college, the deep outside throw is the hardest to complete and many quarterbacks at the lower levels struggle to get the ball to the receiver, especially if it is hash to far boundary. Defensive coaches know the fade route is a tough route to throw, and many offenses would much rather throw a post or slant (more accurate and less time in the air). Like three-point shooting teams in basketball, it can be feast or famine.

The point of a match quarters defense is to bracket the easiest throws (routes by the slot) and force the offense to throw the toughest throws (fades and comebacks). In the lower levels of football, very few quarterbacks can accurately throw from hash to opposite boundary, running match quarters forces these outside throws the offense is trying to eliminate. Spinning on the other hand, puts the dropper and opposite linebacker (both over-hangs) in conflict.

Defending the Modern Spread Offense

"There is no such thing as bad weather, only inappropriate clothing." – German Proverb

--

The traditional tactics of defensive football are being challenged on a daily basis. Maybe not since the advent of the forward pass has defensive football been so challenged. Football is changing. Adapt or die.

--

The run/pass option has inflicted mayhem on traditional defensive theory. No longer can a defense align in any way it pleases, or send risky overload blitzes. The defense must protect every passing lane, and control every gap. Many high school and collegiate defenses are moving to a two-high quarters scheme to combat spread RPO offenses. With a "static" two-high look, the defense is forcing the quarterback to read post-snap, and eliminating the check-with-me offensive coordinator (when the whole offenses freezes and looks to the sideline to get a new play).

Running a two-high scheme allows the defense to gain

cover downs (overhang aligns tighter to the slot) and protects itself in the run game. Where RPO offenses take what the defense gives it, match quarters defenses mirror that thinking defensively. The beauty of a split field two-high scheme is in the flexibility and simplicity of the coverage.

Split coverage schemes are innately simple and align themselves quickly. These fundamental values make it the perfect defense to attack the spread RPO offense, especially ones that utilizes tempo. An extra step that more quarters defenses are using is pressing the corners to deter the RPO hitches and screens, as talked about in the previous chapter. Another way modern defenses are defending RPO offenses is by setting the front to the back. This allows the defense to gain a cover down on the read-side (back's side) slot and thus eliminates the bubble screen, or "pop" pass pre-snap read.

Quarters coverage allows a defense to balance itself and adjust to any formation the offense may throw at it. Many defensive coordinators choose to drop down a safety so the inside linebackers (Mike and Will) can align in the box. There are many ways to gain a six-man box without spinning. Quarters teams use the safeties as extra fitters allowing the safeties to read and react to the play in front of them, correcting the fit of the linebackers.

The old school, Split 4-4, really is antiquated. Even Saban has changed his tone when defending spread teams. Many know Saban as a 3-4 single-high defensive guru, but in recent years (since A&M and Ole Miss started running the spread at elite levels), he has had to switch to a 4-3 two-high look. When a defensive coach does not know where the offense will attack, the best thing to do is be as safe and efficient as possible. The Over Front matched with quarters coverage allows a defense to cover all possible gaps, and protect against the pass by bracketing the seam zone. Want to defeat an RPO team? Force them to hand the ball off. Eliminate the RPO altogether by alignment.

--

The Over Front

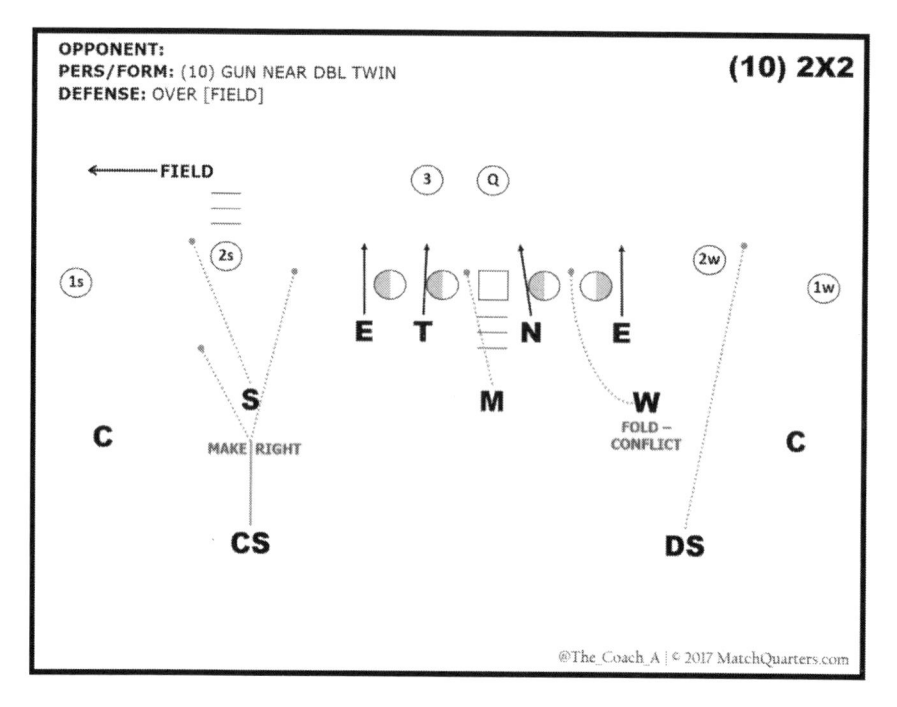

```
OPPONENT:
PERS/FORM: (10) GUN NEAR DBL TWIN                        (10) 2X2
DEFENSE: OVER [FIELD]
```

As offenses continue to push defensive schemes to the brink, it is interesting to note that the oldest of defensive formations, the 4-3 Over Front (above), is coming back into vogue. The Over Front allows defensive coaches to protect their coverage to the field with a cover down, yet maintain gap sound principles in the box. Adding a hybrid player as Sam, or strong side linebacker, can allow a coach to gain an extra coverage man without sacrificing the run fits.

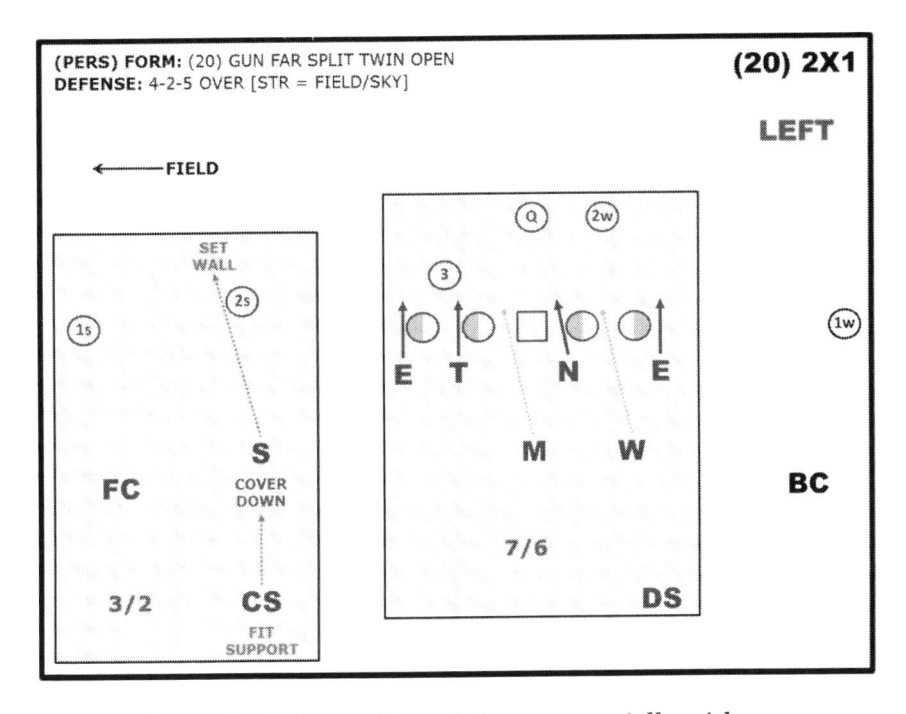

```
(PERS) FORM: (20) GUN FAR SPLIT TWIN OPEN          (20) 2X1
DEFENSE: 4-2-5 OVER [STR = FIELD/SKY]
                                                    LEFT
←———FIELD

                          Q    2w
              SET
              WALL    3
          2s        |O |O □ |O O|         1w
 1s                 E  T    N    E
                         M    W
         S
 FC    COVER                              BC
       DOWN
                      7/6
 3/2    CS                         DS
       FIT
       SUPPORT
```

The goal of the 4-3 Over defense, especially with a hybrid/Nickel defender at Sam, is to have a plus one in the run fits and in pass distribution (see above). Defensive coaches gain numbers in the box by using the Over Front. The front protects a defense's Sam, allowing him to cover down to the slot with no box responsibility. This cover down takes the Sam completely out of the box fits and allows him to focus on his pass responsibilities and defending against RPO screens and pop passes. The Will, or weak-side linebacker, is the defense's fold player, or conflicted player. By putting the fold player to the boundary, the defense can get the best of both worlds. The Will now has enough space to play coverage while also attacking his gap against run. The Mike, or middle linebacker, protects the strong side "A" gap and reacts off the Nose ("G" or 2i) in front of him.

To most offensive coaches, this defensive formation gives the illusion of a "4-1 box." Using this scheme, a defensive coach can play off what RPO spread teams rely on, pre-snap reads. Most spread teams have built in reads dictated by the numbers in the box. With the Sam and Will removed it gives the illusion that there is a five-on-six advantage for the offense. By folding in the Will, and the Sam protecting the outside gap ("O" gap) to the field, the defense is really playing with a seven-man box. By matching quarters coverage behind the front a coach can add two more players to the box (the safeties) without losing his coverage.

Quarters coverage allows the safeties to be ultra-aggressive. Safeties sit at 10 yards and read the #2 receiver through to the tackles. Their main link to the front is the outside linebacker to their side. In the diagram on the previous page, the Cover Safety (CS) relates to the Sam, and the Down Safety (DS) relates to the Will. Against a run to the field, the Sam will try and set a wall by crossing the face of the slot. The CS will then read the Sam and either fit inside or outside depending on the success of the Sam. To the boundary, the DS will fit in the "O" gap. By running this scheme behind the front, a defense can have nine in the box. Here is a diagram of the Over Front defending the most basic spread play, the read option:

To the field -

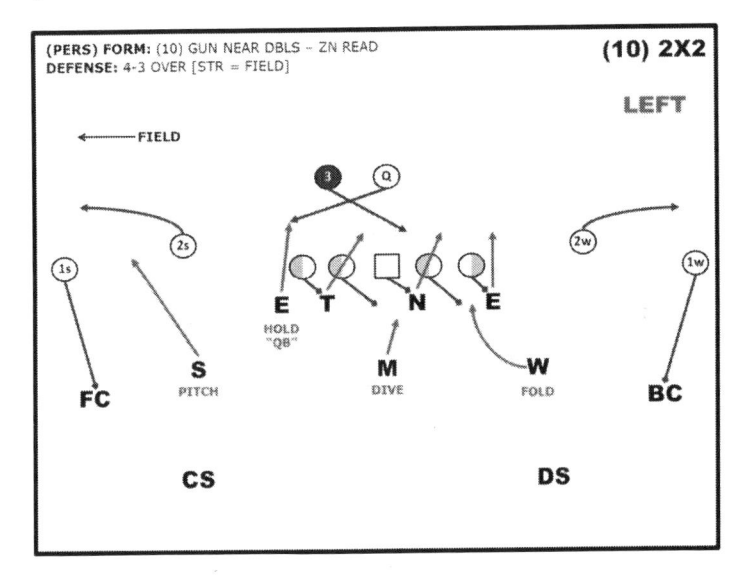

To the boundary –

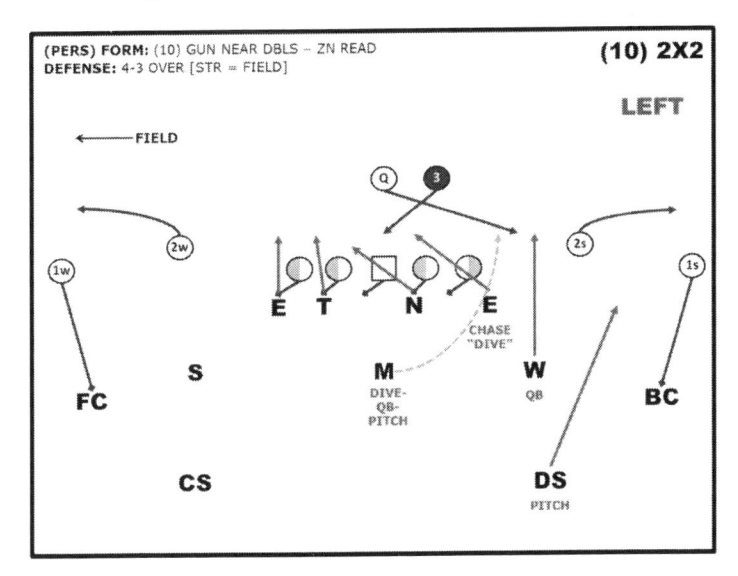

Spinning to single-high creates a void to the single reciever side. Offenses want to throw the most efficient passes they can. Many times this is seen in a hitch or slant to the backside wide receiver. When teams spin a safety down, they are eliminating the help to the single receiver corner, in most cases to the boundary. This leaves the corner on an island. If the corner presses, he is susceptible to the fade with no help. If the corner is soft (six-seven yards deep), the defense is open to RPO/play-action hitches and slants.

Keeping a two-high structure allows the safety to insert in the run, and hang in the curl versus the pass. The boundary safety's alignment helps protect against an RPO offense's opportunity to gain quick efficient throws. The backside choice route, especially vertical, can be devastating to a single-high team (see Baylor under Briles play any single-high team). The middle safety will never be able to make a play to the boundary, so why create that issue. The best way to defend against a team that option routes their boundary single receiver is to stay two-high (and a defense can play with the leverage of the corner and safety). The run fits are cleaner too.

Defending Run/Pass Options

"The essence of strategy is choosing what not to do." – Michael Porter

--

When facing a spread team that RPOs, it is important to understand where the offense wants the ball to go and eliminating that from their play sheet. Strategy, like the quotes suggests, is choosing the path of least resistance. Eliminate the obvious and force the offense to be left handed.

--

The best offenses are chameleons. In the past, in order to change and adapt, an offense had to have a huge grab bag of plays. This created massive playbooks, dense verbiage, and constrictive rules. Just listen to Jon Gruden go through a play call, it is like a mini paragraph. Now turn around and teach that to a 15, 18, or 20-year-old player. NFL teams structure their play calls by telling each individual player what they will do on each play. This style of play calling creates long, wordy phrases and restricts the speed of the game. Offenses that run a multitude of plays become masters at nothing, especially when dealing with the lower level player. Limit the plays, create mastery, and the offense can move at lightning speed. Everyone associated with football knows the term, "Speed Kills". In offense, this can mean explosive plays, defenses off balance, and players streaking untouched into the end zone. The question now is how do defenses catch up?

At the lower levels of football, these dense playbooks do not make sense. Over the past two decades, the spread has developed to fit the unique needs of the lower level coach. Starting in the air-raid Leach offense, with playbooks on a wrinkled piece of paper, to the spread option attacks of Rich Rodriguez and Urban Meyer, the spread has exploded and is revolutionizing America's game. The latest epoch change in the development of spread football is packaged plays, or RPO's. With one play call, an offensive coordinator has several ways to attack the defense, playing off what the defense gives them. By packaging plays an offense, theoretically, can never be wrong. That puts a lot of pressure on the modern defensive coordinator.

--

What is an RPO?

Run/Pass Option, or RPO, has revolutionized the game of football. Offenses at all levels have made a feast on opposing defenses while becoming simpler and faster. The proliferation of spread has even reached the highest level of football. NFL teams are now using simple RPOs to confuse defenses and create an advantage. The age of the inches thick playbook, with hundreds of diagrams filled with dense offensive jargon, are gone. Many teams do not even have playbooks. Teams are shedding the "weight" to gain an advantage on the field. As offensive coaches ditch the playbook and look to gain efficiency and speed, they cut the fat out of their playbooks, trimming verbiage and redundant plays. In a sense, speeding the game up.

The dilemma in cutting plays is the offense can become predictable in nature. To counteract this fact, offenses speed the game up by running play after play with little time as possible between the snaps and changing the formations they use from week to week. As the spread developed, offensive coaches realized that by creating tempo, the offense can actually make the defense predictable. The speed of the offense puts pressure on the defense to line up in the same alignment every time and thus reacting the same way every time. There is nothing sweeter for a coach than to know exactly how an opponent will react. As long as the quarterback makes the right read, an RPO team can slash a defense, create disorder for defensive players, and frustrate the defensive coordinator. Add the fact that the offensive line blocks as though it is a run on every play and the offense has put most the defense in a run-pass conflict. Now, more than ever, defensive coordinators must have sound, efficient defenses.

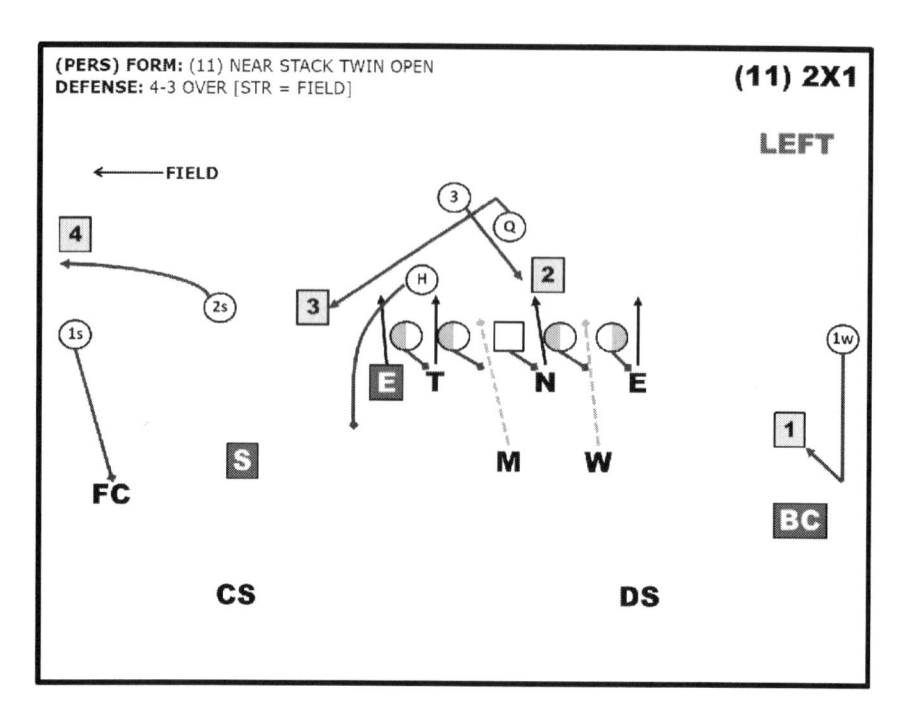

--

```
(PERS) FORM: (11) NEAR STACK TWIN OPEN              (11) 2X1
DEFENSE: 4-3 OVER [STR = FIELD]
                                                    LEFT
```

Simple RPOs like the one above read a defense's alignment pre-snap. In a typical two-back set, an offense can run four plays. Starting to the boundary, the offense reads the leverage of the corner. In most RPO offenses, the backside wide receiver runs a hitch if the corner is deep and a vertical route if the corner is in press. If the boundary corner is off, the quarterback will read this and throw the quick hitch. This is a quick five yards, and no different from a run. It also forces a one-on-one tackling situation for the corner. If the corner misses the tackle, it could be a "house call." To the field, the QB has three options. He can hand the ball off to the running back on a zone run, pull the ball and take off (Zone Read), or throw a quick screen to the receivers to the field (Bubble/Switch). The offense has accomplished this by reading only a few defenders and the leverage of the defense (box numbers). In a perfect world, an offensive coach can call the same play repeatedly, and get a different result on every play.

--

Changing the "B" Gap

How can a defense with limited talent contain an explosive offense that relies heavily on the RPOs? Move the "B" gap. By moving the defensive line the defense stresses the offense's blocking schemes post-snap and changes the expected read for the quarterback. RPO teams rely heavily on pre-snap reads. By moving the gaps after the snap of the ball, a defense can change the read, and can confuse the QB. Hesitation is deadly for any timing offense and creates turnovers.

When designing a defense it is important to start with the run fits first. Most offenses understand running the ball wins games. The run-pass conflict is where teams gain explosive plays by using their lineman as bait. Every defensive coach in the country has argued about offensive linemen downfield. By always firing off the line, and giving a "low hat" (run) read, it draws the defense's linebackers closer to the line of scrimmage, opening passing lanes. If a defensive coordinator sells out on the run, the offense uses the aggressiveness, and the open passing lanes, to blow the top off. The next play, the coordinator could sell out for a sack using an aggressive zone blitz and forget to fill the "A" gap, only to watch the running back scamper untouched up the middle on a simple zone play. These run/pass conflicts are what RPO teams rely on to gain their advantage. Add tempo, and the defense is on their heels.

Defenses can counteract the offenses conflict reads by using line movement to change the gaps and the defense's structure post-snap. Look at the top defenses in college football and there is a trend. Most colleges are implementing some version of a split field match quarters scheme. What is the new in vogue defense to run, the old school 4-3 Over Front.

Most spread teams want to attack the open gap and play off the run-pass conflict created by this natural opening. Whether it is whole line movements, or just moving the interior defensive line, by moving the gaps a defense changes its shape and structure leading to muddy reads and hesitation in a rhythm offense. An

RPO team relies on precise reads by the QB. When an RPO team adds tempo, a defense has to line up and get simple. As stated earlier, simple can mean predictability, and in football, predictability gets you beat.

Using gap exchange post-snap can cause hesitation by the QB. Hesitation in football means mistakes. Look at any top team in the country and they usually have a staggering plus turnover margin. Mistakes by an offense lead to turnovers. Creating doubt in a QB can derail any explosive offense. Simple line movements, or exotic stunts, it does not matter. As long as a defense can simply change the read and the gaps post-snap, an RPO offense will struggle. See diagrams on the next page.

Here are examples of line movement changing the reads:

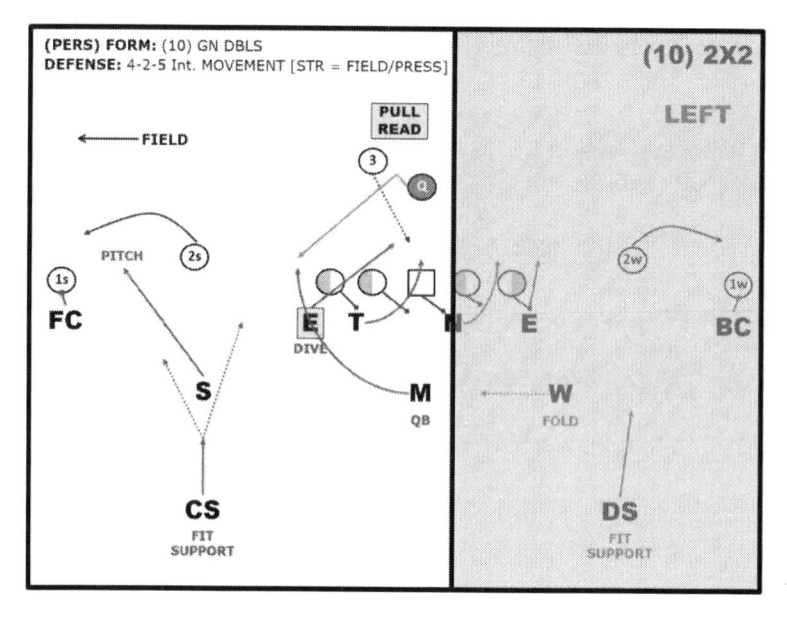

Interior movement changes the read from a "give" to a "pull."

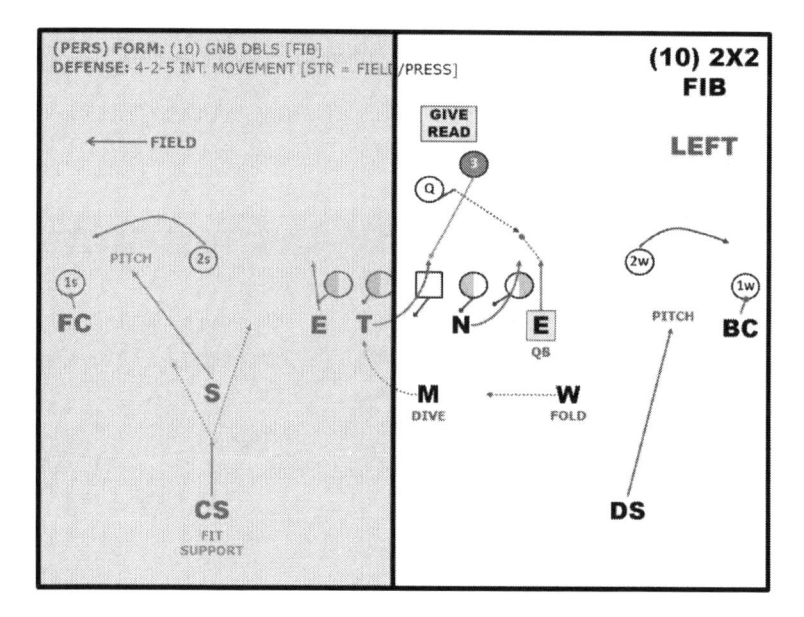

In the diagram above, the opposite is the case. The same movement creates a "give" read.

Attacking the Tendencies

All offenses have tendencies. In order to determine what type of line movement to use, a defensive coach must determine where the offense wants the ball to go (inside or outside) and who is their greatest running threat, the RB or QB. Coverage wise, is the quick screen their go-to for the RPO, or is the offense trying to get their stud "X" (single) receiver to the boundary on a hitch or vertical? Once a defense has a tendency, it can play on the reads.

Maybe the defense has a stud Mike, and the offense wants to make him wrong every time, change his gap responsibility and move him around. The offense can also read the leverage of the safety in order to determine the receiver's route, play quarters and change the coverage on the single receiver side from Cover Two, to Cover Four, to man. A defense must always be gap sound, and have a backup plan if the offense takes advantage of the defensive scheme. Move the interior line one play to change the cover down, then full line movement the next play to get the QB to pull the ball. All these examples are ways a defense can play with an offense's reads pre- and post-snap.

Another way defenses can gain an edge on an RPO offense is to formation their blitzes and alignments. Not every blitz, line movement, or even coverage, will work against every formation. If there were an umbrella defense, everyone would run it. Even Rex Ryan, in a press conference, before he played the "spread guru" Chip Kelly's scheme of check-with-me remarked that, "all teams in college are just going to run quarters." Well, there is a reason. Offenses have the advantage at the lower levels of football, and the antiquated days of putting your best players on defense are long gone. The NFL is about man match-ups and defeating pass protection.

Playing man is easy, but not everyone has the depth to man up across the board. This is why quarters coverage is gaining traction as a base defense at the lower levels of football. Modern defenses at the armature level have to rely on lesser athletes to get production against explosive offenses using schemes that spread them out and play off traditional run-pass rules.

--

Base Run Fits

Against a power team, the tendency is to spin to single-high. The issues that arise from this thinking are what to do when a team has a stud receiver, and can an offense max-protect. The single-high safety in the middle of the field cannot make a play on a single receiver close to the boundary. It becomes a one-on-one matchup with the corner. The offense wants a defense to spin. By spinning, the defense is eliminating angles. Spin down a safety and a defense will lose a man in the box because he cannot reach the field on an outside play away. Spinning also overloads a side if spinning strong. The best way to protect a defense against the power cutback is to hold the boundary safety (DS) high so he can insert and make the Will right (cutback/reverse). See the fits versus power below.

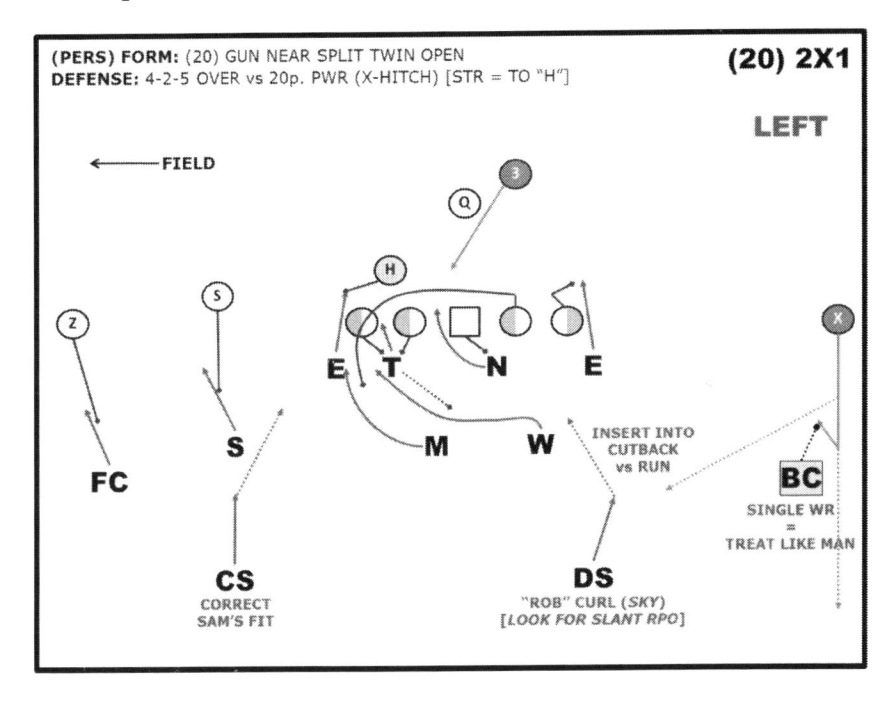

(PERS) FORM: (20) GUN NEAR SPLIT TWIN OPEN
DEFENSE: 4-2-5 OVER vs 20p. PWR (X-HITCH) [STR = TO "H"]

(20) 2X1
LEFT

← FIELD

INSERT INTO CUTBACK vs RUN

BC
SINGLE WR = TREAT LIKE MAN

FC

CS
CORRECT SAM'S FIT

DS
"ROB" CURL (SKY)
[LOOK FOR SLANT RPO]

The DS at his regular quarters position has the opportunity to clearly see the cutback and help the Will. If the Will is pinned, he can correct his error. By spinning the DS to the boundary, the defense loses a man in the run fit, and the safety can easily be caught in trash so close to the line and outside the perimeter of the box.

Against 11/20 personnel teams, spinning lends a defense to be susceptible to the backside choice route and vertical passing game. When facing a 10 personnel team, the defense gains a defender in the box by spinning a safety, but stresses both seam players. Spinning in the middle of the field leaves the corners on islands, and stresses the deep safety (middle third/high-hole). If the centerfield safety guesses wrong on defending a seam route the offense can easily go the other way (all a QB has to do is look off the high safety). Defenses should fight the urge to spin versus two-back. The offense wants the defense to have that reaction. On paper, it may make sense to add a box player when the offense adds a back, but the game of football is about angles, and leaving two safeties with depth helps the defense stay plus-one in both the run and pass.

--

There is a reason more college and high school programs are turning to the 4-3/4-2 hybrid quarters scheme. It just makes sense. With lesser athletes, a defense can compress the offense, and force less productive throws. When playing teams that throw vertical, it is important to remember, it is not about eliminating the big play; it is about surviving them. Michigan St. hung with Baylor's onslaught of deep balls in the 2014 Cotton Bowl, knowing that eventually the offense would miss a few times and get behind the chains (much like 3-point teams have streaks during a game). The system of patience worked. If a defense is outmatched athletically, do not make it worse by playing man. Spinning puts more pressure on more players and creates one-on-one matchups across the board. Stay Two-High.

Cody Alexander

Systematic Creativity of a Quarters Defense

"There's less room for trying [stuff], and more of an emphasis on doing the right [stuff]." – Bruce Arena, USMNT Head Coach

--

This quote is referring to the debate between over ultra-aggressive attacking style of modern soccer (think blitz-centric single-high) versus systems that base in keeping a solid structure and attacking at appropriate times (two-high quarters). Though the quote is about soccer, it holds true in American football as well. Quarters is not about doing a lot of "stuff," it is about doing things in a structured manner.

--

Everyone loves a home run; the power, the violence, and the glory that comes when a batter swings for the fences and connects. It is a visceral reaction. Teams that blitz on every down, spin the secondary on every snap, and fly to the ball are entertaining to watch. The physical nature of a blitz is thrilling. There is no doubt why many coaches turn to zone blitzing, adding men to the box by spinning and playing an ultra-attack style defense. It is aesthetically pleasing too. Don Brown, the defensive coordinator for Michigan, in an interview after giving up several big plays against lesser spread opponents in UCF and Colorado in 2016 had this to say about quarters, *"[Offenses] want you to line up in quarters and a static front and kick your you-know-what. We're not doing that... We're going to stay aggressive, we're going to stay focused, and we're going to stay multiple."* It would be hard to find an interview where Narduzzi, Dantonio, Patterson, or Phil Bennett, all quarters gurus, refer to their defenses as cautious and timid.

Every defensive coach should have Don Brown's mentality. Being static does get a defense beat. Lining up the same way, every play... gets you beat. This is something that most defensive coaches know and understand. Ian Boyd, writer for *Football Study Hall* and *SportsTreatise.com*, stated, *"Gary Patterson's brand of quarters at TCU was revolutionary for the way it used split field coverages to create more complexity with greater simplicity for the players..."* By splitting the field, a defense opens the door for a more complex, yet simple system.

In the age of up-tempo spread offenses, a defense has to be multiple, flexible, and simple at the same time. Blitzing 60+ percent of the time, throwing guys in multiple positions, and rolling the secondary on every play is fun to watch (see the NFL's viewer numbers), but it also gives up tons of big plays (especially if you do not have the athletes to play man). When a team has superior talent, a blitz-centric style of defense can easily overpower a weaker foe because they can win the one-on-one match-ups. It is when ultra-aggressive defenses face a good-to-elite spread team that spaces them out and challenges the defense one-on-one across the board that we see cracks in a defense's armor. Defending the modern spread is about being systematically sound in the structure of a defense, while being creative and adaptive within the established base to cause confusion for the offense.

True split field quarters coverage schemes are about getting gap sound, lining up the right way, and then attack the offense with slight adjustments and pressures. Everyone loves Mike Tyson from his prime; brash, violent, and strong. Think of single-high blitz-centric defenses as Mike Tyson. When a defense like that has superior athletes they dominate, when they face an even foe, they tire and wear down. The big plays get more noticeable, and the score is much higher.

Elite quarters teams are like Floyd Mayweather. They defend themselves against the big punch, and if one lands, they keep plugging away because it was not a knock out shot; they did not expose themselves to a fatal blow by the offense. Quarters defenses are able to defend themselves against bigger, stronger foes without losing an edge. It is *cautious aggression*. The scheme is defensive, but when the time is right, the defense takes its shots.

Do quarters teams get lit up? Yes, but the argument of two-high versus single-high is not about that, both can be beat. Quarters teams make an offense earn it. It really boils down to a choice: 1) Compress the opponent, make them work for every yard and take shots when they are open; or 2) Throw haymakers and hope a defense can land a knock-out punch early, but in the case of #2, if the defense misses, they get knocked out. There is a defense for every situation; some are just safer and more efficient than others are.

--

Blitzing from a Two-Shell

The word static is used a great deal when talking about quarters coverage. In football terms, the word refers to the alignment of the defense. The belief that quarters teams line up the same way every down is true to an extent, but it is what happens after the play that really defines the creativity in the coverage schemes.

Most match quarters teams split the field. By doing so, the defense is making the alignment of the offense more predictable. If broken down, the offense can only line up in so many sets (2x2, 3x1, 2x1, 1x1, and 4x1). Divide this by two (splitting the field) and a defense reduces that number even more. Allowing the safeties to work independently also allows a defensive coordinator to get creative. Where blitz-centric teams must spin to single-high and replace a blitzer, split field teams can turn to man principles on one side, and retain their zone structure on the other half of the field.

Teams like to throw hot routes into the blitz because there is a void left where the blitzer came from. The attempt to cover this void is where you get the theory of zone blitzing; send pressure then sling a linebacker or defensive linemen to the void created by the vacating blitzers. The problem with zone blitzing is many times the defense can get out of alignment, or sucked in on play-action. Man blitzing teams are able to send more than the offensive line can handle while keeping its pass integrity. Keeping a man shell behind a blitz allows a team to absorb verticals, and drive on hot routes, like "Sticks" coverage (a coverage where the secondary players align on or near the first down line). The objective of blitzing with a man shell is to eliminate the quick throw for the offense, allowing the blitz to hit every time.

Split field quarters teams are best suited for man blitzing because of the coverage shell. The "static" alignment of the secondary allows the defense to look the same even when blitzing. This also creates opportunities to bluff, or show blitz with the linebackers. Bluffing can be a great tool against "check-with-me" offenses. At the snap of the ball, the offense cannot tell if there is a blitz or the defense is just showing they are coming. Teams that spin must show early so they do not get out of alignment and the spinning safety can get in position. It is easier for a secondary player to defend from depth than to work backwards against a vertical. Spinning while blitzing opens up the defense to quick vertical throws. Playing man behind a blitz enables the secondary to drive on hot routes (hitches/slants) and absorb vertical routes.

--

The Trips Dilemma

Trips formations (3x1) tend to give zone blitz/single-high teams problems because the third receiver makes the defense rotate, allowing the Mike to work back into the box. This is where split field teams have an advantage. To keep a six-man box and eliminate the run/pass conflict for the Mike, single-high teams rotate to the three-receiver side. Though spinning takes the Mike out of conflict, this secondary movement locks the backside corner on the single receiver with no help. The diagram below demonstrates a basic Cover 3 look. By kicking the safety to the #3 receiver, the defense has rotated to the strength. Doing this exposes not only the boundary corner to a one-on-one match-up but to any weakside run as well.

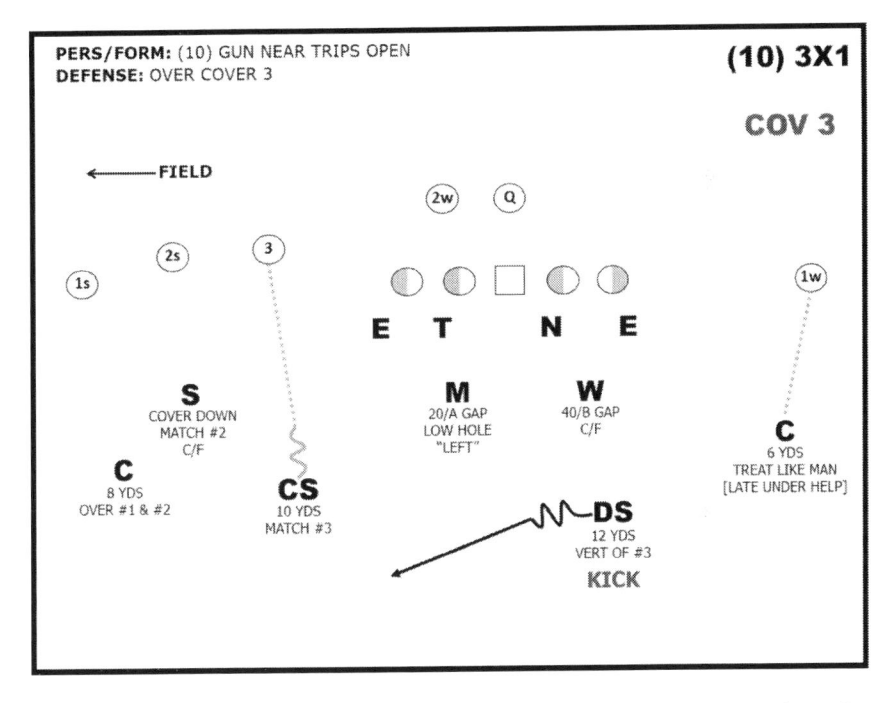

```
PERS/FORM: (10) GUN NEAR TRIPS OPEN        (10) 3X1
DEFENSE: OVER COVER 3
                                            COV 3
```

Diagram: (10) Gun Near Trips Open vs. Over Cover 3

- S — COVER DOWN, MATCH #2, C/F
- M — 20/A GAP, LOW HOLE, "LEFT"
- W — 40/B GAP, C/F
- C (field) — 8 YDS, OVER #1 & #2
- CS — 10 YDS, MATCH #3
- DS — 12 YDS, VERT OF #3, KICK
- C (boundary) — 6 YDS, TREAT LIKE MAN [LATE UNDER HELP]

The point of keeping a two-high shell is to stay balanced, and keep a plus one in pass distribution and run fits. Kicking the safety to the field eliminates a man to the weak side. Against a gap scheme offense (power/counter/fold), the offense has a man-on-man advantage. The boundary safety kicking to the field will be late on any run away from the Trips side. If the safety misses an open field tackle or does not run the alley, it is a touchdown. Many coaches spin to keep a six-man box, by doing this they eliminate a boundary defender and leave themselves vulnerable.

Split field teams are able to change the way they play Trips from series to series or game to game depending on what the offense gives them. Single-high teams have two choices, spin to the Trips, or spin away from the Trips. Either way, they are tipping off the offense by rolling. The "static" quarters look allows the defense to hold their structure longer, and force the offense to guess what is coming. Essentially, the defense is making a 17/18 year old kid beat them and not an offensive coordinator.

Don Brown's argument that he wants teams checking to the sideline because that allows him to dictate tempo has a point, but the offense does not mind because it allows them to get into a play they feel comfortable with, while the defense shows the offense where the pressure is coming from. Even if the defense changes after the check to the sideline, the offense still knows where the defense's pass distribution is because the safeties have rotated.

In the diagram on the next page, a two-high scheme allows the defense the luxury of staying balanced versus a 3x1 formation.

Single-high coaches and offensive coordinators will argue that Mike is in conflict, and he is, but the defensive structure is much safer.

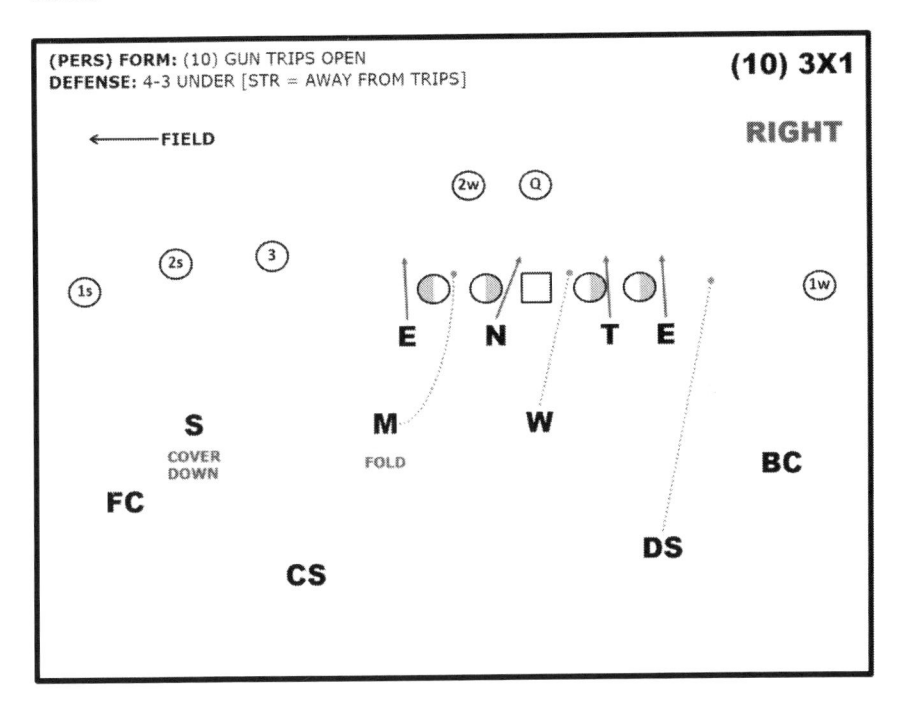

```
(PERS) FORM: (10) GUN TRIPS OPEN                    (10) 3X1
DEFENSE: 4-3 UNDER [STR = AWAY FROM TRIPS]
                                                    RIGHT
   ←——— FIELD

                        (2w)  (Q)

         (2s)  (3)
   (1s)              | ● ● □ ● ● |               (1w)
                       E  N   T  E

            S          M        W
         COVER       FOLD                       BC
         DOWN
      FC
                                       DS
                CS
```

If teams begin to roll to the three-receiver side, offenses change their RPO to the "X" receiver. Most quarters coaches would rather the offense throw a quick strike to the #3 receiver, with help over the top, then throw a slant or fade off play-action to a one-on-one corner. If the offense connects, it is a huge gain or even a touchdown.

The main objective of a two-high shell is to create even distribution, and force the quarterback to throw the least percentage throw (deep and outside). A quarters defense forces the offense to change or work to reach open receivers.

--

The Pseudo Single-High

Against two-back teams, a quarters defense is able to stay even, attack strong and weak, while also protecting against the cutback. Aligning against a 21 personnel set, quarters reacts much the same way teams that spin, but without the over rotation. The alignment by quarters defenses allows them to attack the offense with *cautious aggression*. Against two running backs quarters defenses are pseudo single-high. In the diagram below, a quarters scheme allows the field safety to stay high and correct the Mike. The boundary safety sits high and protects from the cutback.

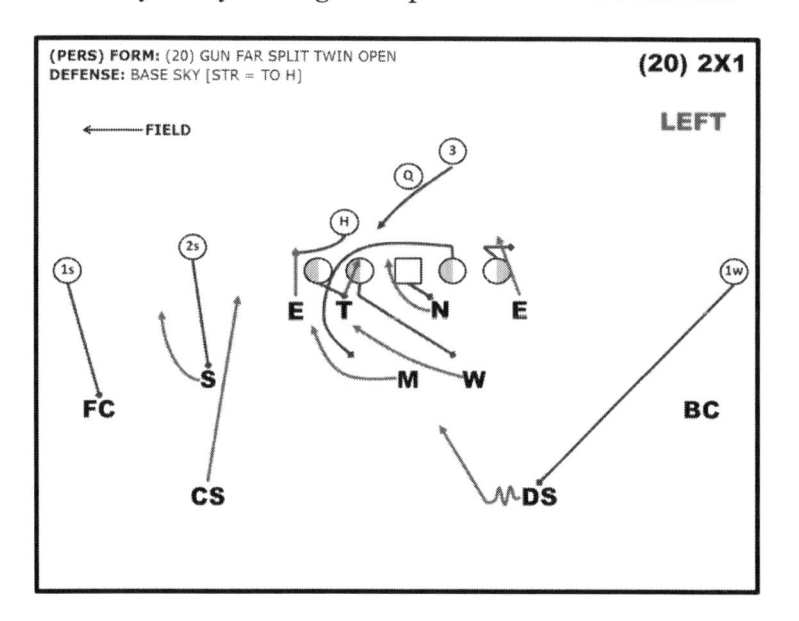

If a defense were to spin to the weak side, the boundary safety has a chance to be caught in trash while he works into the box, or never show up for the cutback. By staying two-high, the defense can gain four players on one pulling guard. Even if the linemen coming off the double team catch the Will, the boundary safety is there to correct him. If spinning to the strength the defense can get over rotated and lose its numbers to the weak side (think counter backside). A two-high look versus a 21 personnel Pro formation allows the defense to rotate with the offensive play and gives the boundary safety a better angle for the cutback (see image).

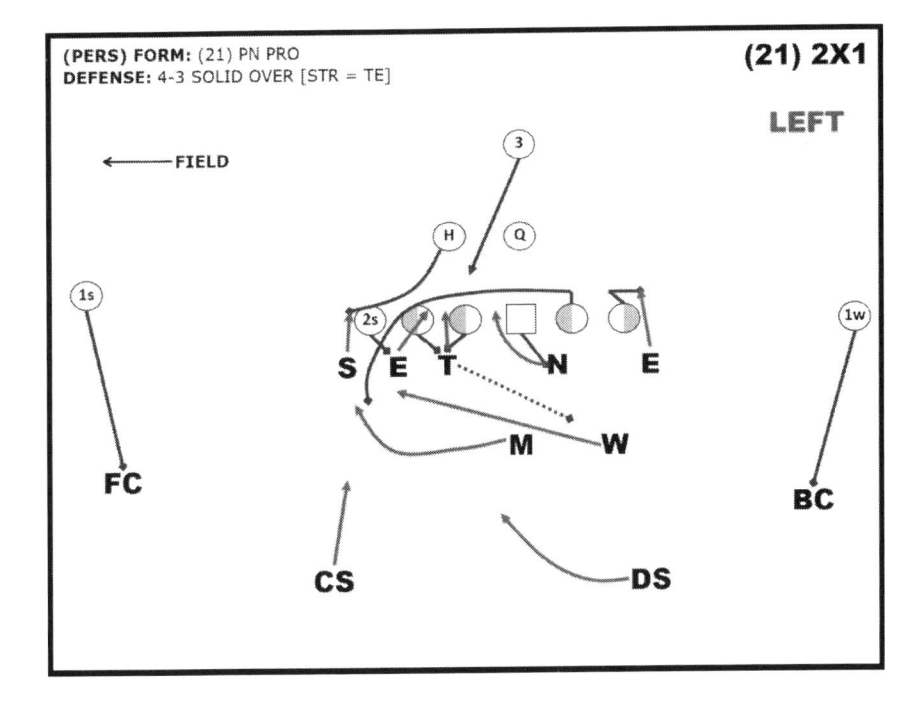

(PERS) FORM: (21) PN PRO
DEFENSE: 4-3 SOLID OVER [STR = TE]

(21) 2X1

LEFT

The same distribution is critical against the trending two-back RPO teams. Offenses that RPO want a defense to rotate (spin) and become unbalanced. If a defense spins to the weakside the offense will throw the hitch to the single receiver or RPO the Sam's leverage on the bubble (two-on-two is still one-on-one). Rotate to the field, and the offense will throw the slant/post to the single receiver ("X"), or flip the back and read the defensive end to the boundary where the defense just vacated their plus one defender (see image below).

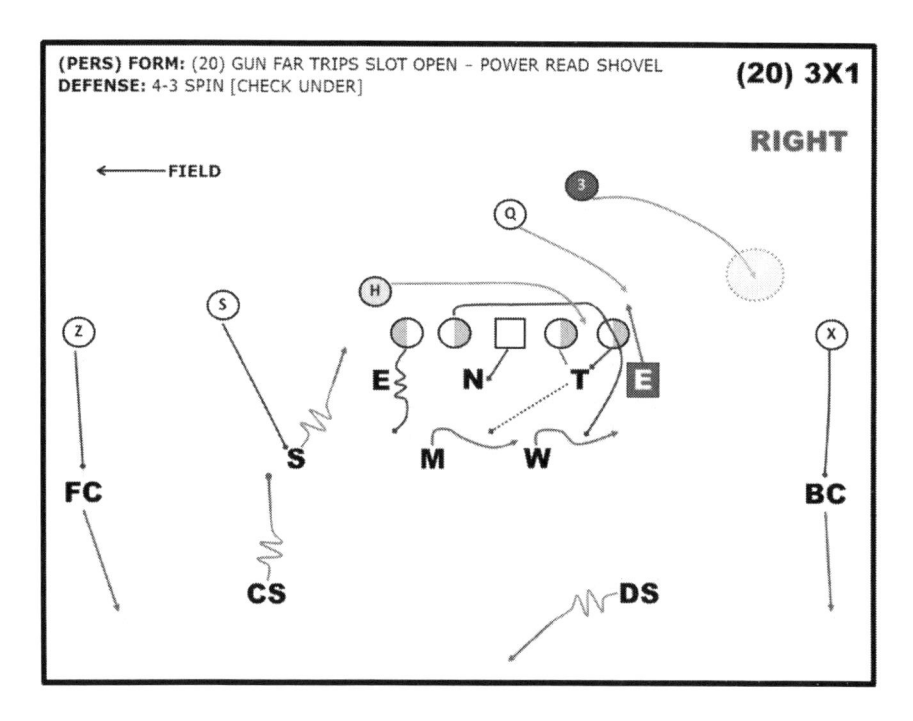

Leveraging the Boundary

The modern spread offense wants to create one-on-one match-ups. Spinning gets the defense off balance. Staying in a two-high shell against spread RPO teams makes the offense search for the open man, or just hand the ball off (predictability). Quarters also gives the defense the ability to create more in the way they attack an RPO offense by constantly changing the "B" gap and leverage of the secondary.

A split field defensive scheme creates two fields. To the boundary, the defensive coordinator can play with the leverage of the corner and the safety. Spinning to single-high forces the field safety to work to the middle of the field, and play from sideline to sideline. In a split field look, a defensive coordinator can walk the boundary safety down and blitz him or drop him underneath the #1 receiver. Against "check-with-me" teams, this look can freeze an offensive coordinator (image on the next page).

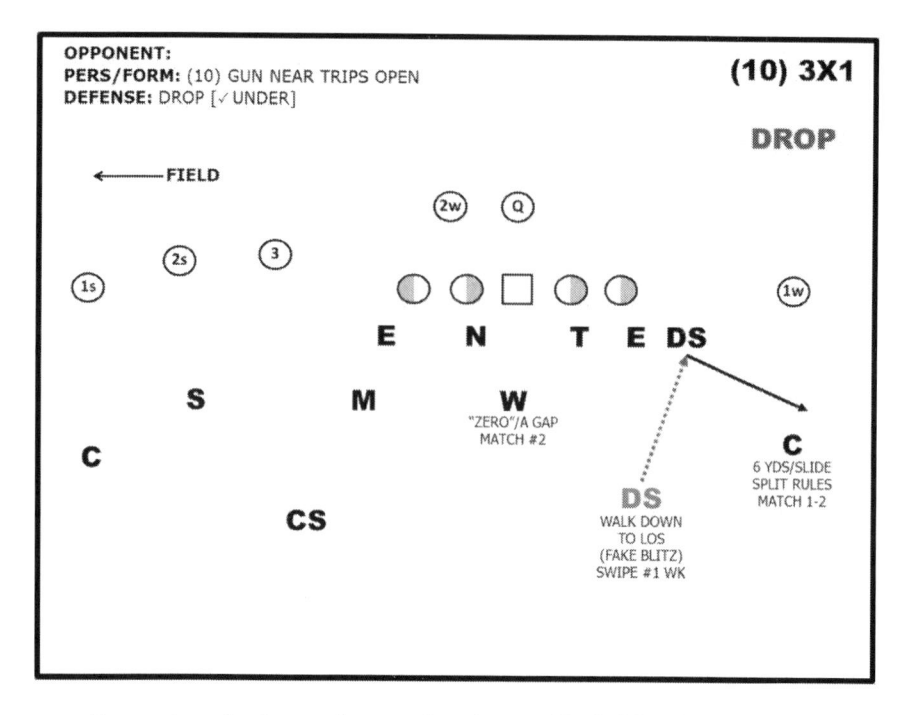

OPPONENT:
PERS/FORM: (10) GUN NEAR TRIPS OPEN
DEFENSE: DROP [✓ UNDER]

(10) 3X1

DROP

◄─── FIELD

```
                    (2w) (Q)
      (2s) (3)
(1s)          ○ ◐ □ ◑ ○           (1w)
               E  N   T  E DS
         S        M      W
                       "ZERO"/A GAP
                       MATCH #2
  C                                        C
                                         6 YDS/SLIDE
                                         SPLIT RULES
                              DS         MATCH 1-2
              CS           WALK DOWN
                            TO LOS
                           (FAKE BLITZ)
                           SWIPE #1 WK
```

Dropping the boundary safety in a split field scheme is no different from what his distribution would be in "Sky" coverage. The safety is underneath all routes and fills the "O" gap on any run. By splitting the field, a defensive coordinator can get a single-high look without spinning. The field safety (CS) stays with his main role to the field (bracketing the slot and correcting the Sam). A defense can do this to a 3x1 set as well.

--

It is also important to point out that a defensive coordinator should not forget the corners when playing with the secondary's leverage to the boundary. Being able to press the single receiver and gain a bracket can eliminate plays from the offensive playbook. One great way to scheme against an RPO teams is to trap your corners. In trap coverage, the corner apexes between the offensive tackle and the single receiver ("X"). This is in essence Cover 2 to the boundary, except, the corner now has better leverage on the run (diagram below).

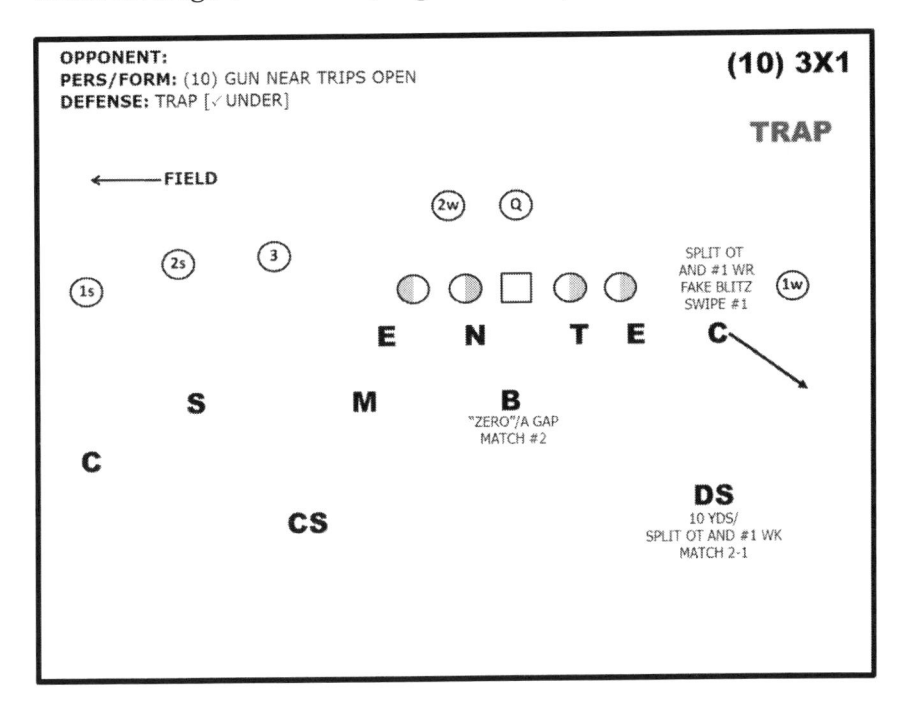

```
OPPONENT:
PERS/FORM: (10) GUN NEAR TRIPS OPEN                    (10) 3X1
DEFENSE: TRAP [✓ UNDER]
                                                        TRAP
        ←—— FIELD
                          (2w)  (Q)
          (2s)  (3)                      SPLIT OT
   (1s)                                  AND #1 WR
                   O  O  □  O  O         FAKE BLITZ   (1w)
                                         SWIPE #1
                   E  N     T  E     C↘

        S         M         B
                         "ZERO"/A GAP
                         MATCH #2
   C
                                              DS
                   CS                       10 YDS/
                                         SPLIT OT AND #1 WK
                                              MATCH 2-1
```

Being able to play with leverage to the single receiver, while keeping the cover down to the field eliminates plays from the offense's playbook, this cannot be said for single-high defenses.

--

Quarters coverage is not boring. Teams that run quarters have a structure that protects them from big plays. Within this structure is the room for vast creativity, maybe even more than what single-high teams can do.

Quarters is safe, yes, but it has its purpose. When teams spin, they lose their leverage away from the dropping safety unless it is an even formation (2x2). It also puts more pressure on the defensive players because they are in more one-on-one situations. If a defense has the athletes to win its one-on-ones then by all means, run single-high, but understand offenses want the defense to spin. Ask any great offensive coordinator and they will say they lick their chops when defenses start spinning.

The creativity allowed in a split field scheme is limitless. Quarters does not have to be boring. Blitzes from a quarters playbook tend to be gap sound and do not lose their pass distribution when blitzing (especially if defense "zero" or man blitzes). The whole premise of a quarters scheme is to be gap sound and bracket the most dangerous receivers, the slots. This is different from single-high. Ask any defensive coach who runs single-high coverage and they will admit the seam is a very dangerous area. The players in charge of that area have to be correct or it is often times fatal.

There is a tendency for single-high teams to be blitz-centric. They rely on the pressure to force bad throws and tackles in the backfield. When single-high teams face good to elite spread teams the scheme can be exposed because of the one-on-one matchups, many times down the seam. Staying in a two-high shell allows teams to compress the field and force the offense to work. A team with lesser talent can hang with athletic juggernauts because they stay gap sound and eliminate the big play.

Quarters is a structured defense. The creativity comes from the movement post snap. Players in a quarters scheme are allowed to keep everything in front of them, and force the offense to change, sometimes eliminating whole packages. It is always easier for a player to work down than to work backwards. That is the beauty within quarters coverage. It is systematic creativity. A defense can blitz, stunt, move the line, or anything else, but by staying two-high, the defense's structure is safer and gap sound. Every defense has its place; some are just safer than others are.

Cody Alexander

The Art of Match Quarters

"The supreme art of war is to subdue the enemy without fighting."
– Sun Tzu, *Art of War*

--

Detractors of the quarters scheme argue that the static nature of the scheme lends itself to exposure by offenses. Quarters is not a static, passive defense, rather a tactical choice to force the offense into low percentage choices. As the quote explains, supremacy is found in manipulation, not brute force.

--

With many spread offenses relying on a "check-with-me" system, it is important for defenses to look the same on every snap. The catch 22 is by staying static the offense is able to predict how the defense will react. Offenses have evolved, especially at the high school and collegiate levels, to read one-half of the field. By doing this, offenses can simplify the terminology (speed up the game/more plays) and attack a defense's weaker players. Defenses that show their cards early are now at a disadvantage. When a defense moves before the snap, an offense is able to "freeze" and look to the sideline (hence the name "check-with-me"). Once the offensive coordinator sees where the defense is going, he can quickly change the play and attack the vulnerabilities shown by the early movement. Add varying offensive formations and splits of the receivers, it can quickly become a nightmare for defensive coordinators.

In order for a defensive coordinator to attack a spread offense, he must think like a spread offense coordinator. This is where splitting the field and playing match coverages can lead to a defensive advantage. A defensive coach can half the field and allow each safety to choose the correct coverage to run behind the base defense. This is much like a quarterback in a spread scheme reading his key on a run/pass option (RPO), or packaged play, and selecting the correct play for what he sees. In a split field concept, the safeties have to be the quarterbacks once the Mike has set the front.

Match quarters uses the old school framework of an Over Cover 4 scheme. In a true Cover 4, the secondary literally splits the field into quarters. Secondary players are responsible for "deeper than the deepest" in their respective field zones. Underneath the secondary, the linebackers drop to spots on the field, the Sam and

Will drop curl-to-flat and the Mike drops to the "low hole" in the middle of the field. The problem with running a true Cover 4 is that the defense is dropping to a spot and not relating to a man. By implementing match schemes, a defense relates to a certain man regardless of formation while keeping the protection of a quarters scheme.

With offenses running multiple formations, it is important for a defensive coordinator to keep the scheme simple yet complex enough to be able to attack an offense, and keep them off guard. By allowing the safeties to dictate the coverage, a defense can be more adaptive and flexible. In match coverage, the scheme is based on the offensive formation, and then the defenders relate to a certain man in that formation. Corners will always relate to the #1 receiver, the safeties, and the outside linebackers will relate to the #2 receivers, and the Mike will always relate to #3. No matter what formation an offense throws at a defense, running match quarters can adjust to it. If a player can count to three then he can play in a match scheme.

--

Sky/Cloud Concepts

Match quarters teams adjust to the formation and splits of the receivers by splitting the field in half then delineating the coverage. Sky is the match version of Cover 4. The term "Sky" tells the safety that he is involved in the run fits, and can be aggressive to the ball. This coverage tells the corner he is playing man on #1, unless the receiver goes underneath "right now." In that case, the corner would climb to the #2 receiver if he is running a corner route (see image below).

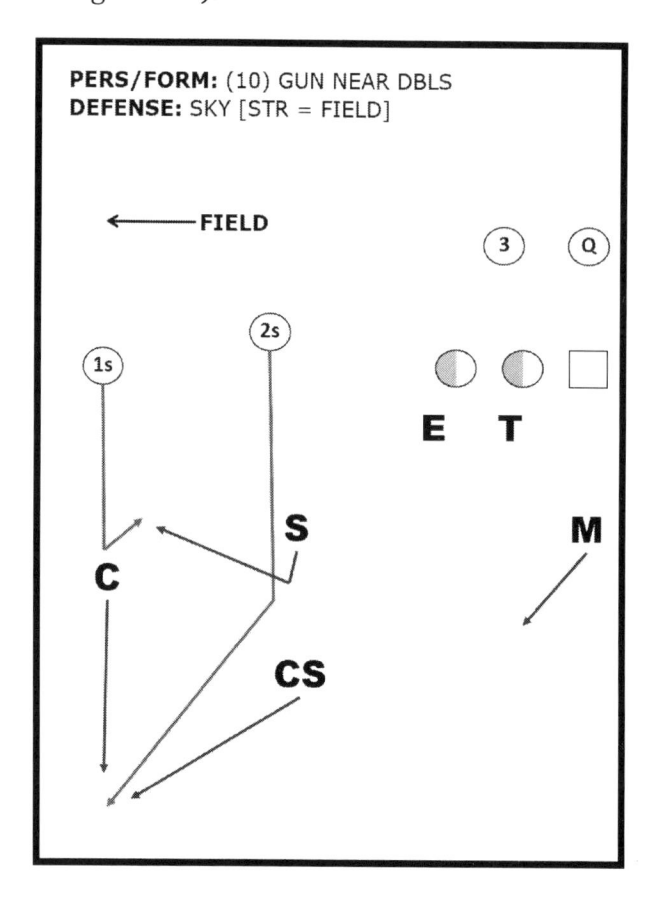

PERS/FORM: (10) GUN NEAR DBLS
DEFENSE: SKY [STR = FIELD]

←——— FIELD

The safety in Sky is allowed to be aggressive against the run and is underneath any vertical route by #1 (intermediate zone). If an offense runs both #1 and #2 receivers vertical, the safety "tops" the route of #2, taking the entire vertical. The outside linebackers in Sky coverage relate to the #2 receiver and do not work outside of him until he is "pushed" (crossed) by another route coming in, or going out. Sky allows the defense to gain a nine-man box by being aggressive with the safeties, as long as #2 does not go vertical. See a diagram of Sky coverage below.

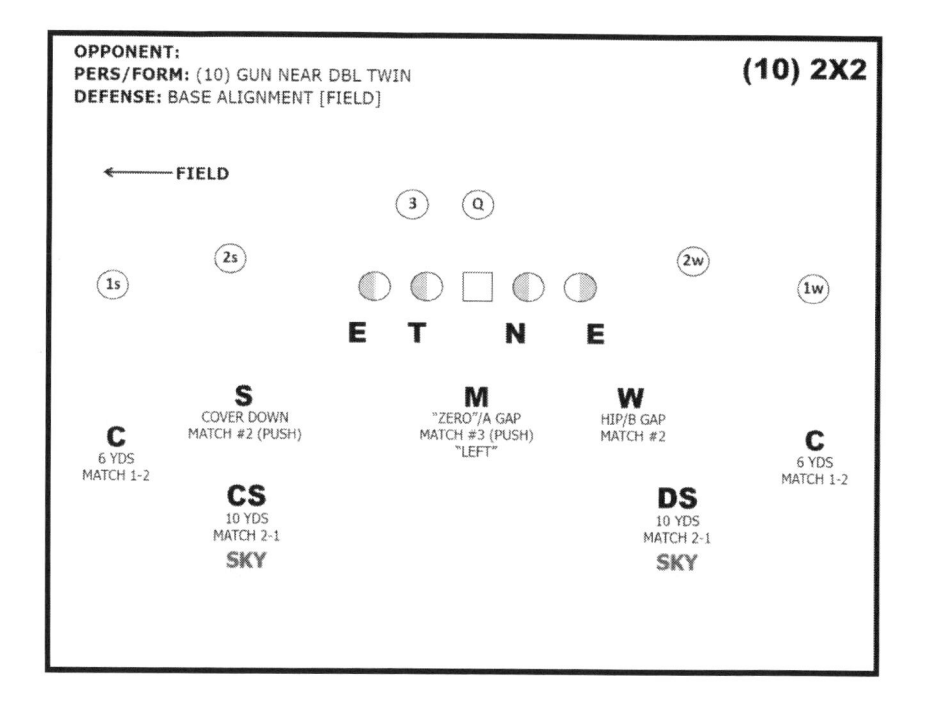

```
OPPONENT:
PERS/FORM: (10) GUN NEAR DBL TWIN                      (10) 2X2
DEFENSE: BASE ALIGNMENT [FIELD]


    ←——— FIELD
                              3    Q
              2s                                2w
    1s                                                 1w
                      ●  ●  □  ●  ●
                      E  T  N  E

              S              M              W
         COVER DOWN     "ZERO"/A GAP     HIP/B GAP
    C    MATCH #2 (PUSH) MATCH #3 (PUSH) MATCH #2       C
   6 YDS                     "LEFT"                    6 YDS
  MATCH 1-2                                          MATCH 1-2
              CS                             DS
             10 YDS                        10 YDS
            MATCH 2-1                     MATCH 2-1
              SKY                            SKY
```

--

- 77 -

Cloud technique is the match version of Cover 2, and the term "Cloud" tells the corners they are involved in the run fits. In Cloud, the corner reacts to any out route by the #2 receiver. The safety in Cloud is in a fast bail, still maintaining inside leverage on #2 until he breaks outside. The outside linebacker will hold the curl, and relate off #2, carrying him vertical and only pushing outside late because he has a corner playing hard on the edge. If the offense sends both #1 and #2 vertical it turns into man-to-man coverage, and the corner absorbs the #1 receiver and carries him vertical. Cloud is diagramed below.

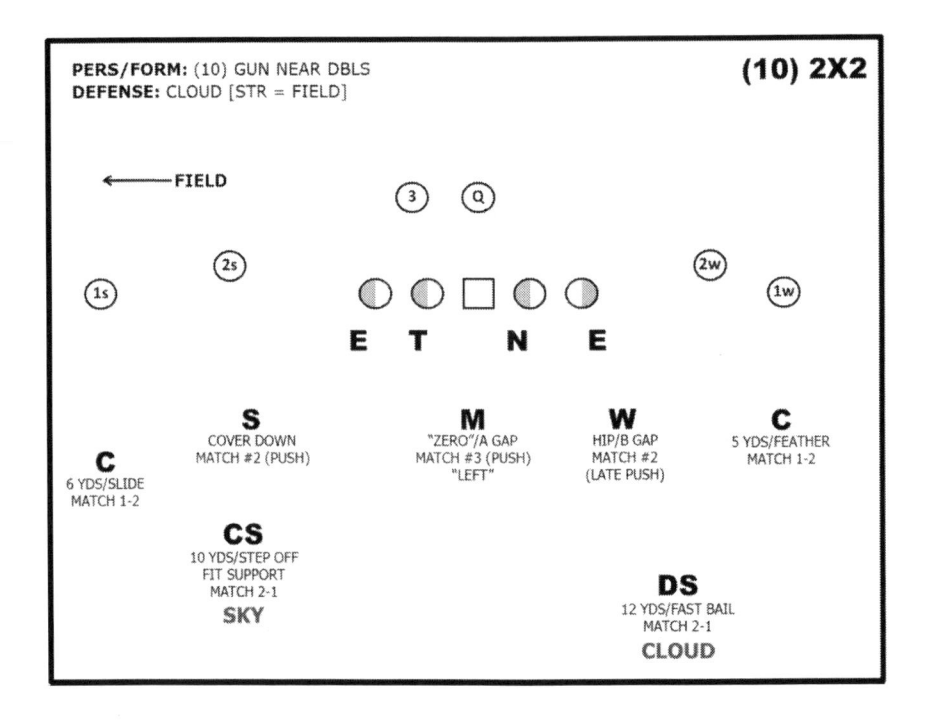

```
PERS/FORM: (10) GUN NEAR DBLS                           (10) 2X2
DEFENSE: CLOUD [STR = FIELD]


    ←——— FIELD              3    Q

                    2s                              2w
          1s                                                1w
                        ○ ○ □ ○ ○
                        E  T  N  E

              S                 M           W           C
           COVER DOWN        "ZERO"/A GAP  HIP/B GAP  5 YDS/FEATHER
     C     MATCH #2 (PUSH)  MATCH #3 (PUSH)  MATCH #2   MATCH 1-2
  6 YDS/SLIDE                  "LEFT"      (LATE PUSH)
   MATCH 1-2
              CS
           10 YDS/STEP OFF
           FIT SUPPORT
           MATCH 2-1                            DS
              SKY                          12 YDS/FAST BAIL
                                             MATCH 2-1
                                               CLOUD
```

Cloud coverage is an answer to the Tampa 2 and "cluster" (close set) dilemma. In Tampa 2 the Mike is asked to "run the pole" or, run down the middle third of the field and defend the high hole (middle third). This scheme can take away the aggressiveness of Mike in the run game, and leave a defense wide open in the middle, and underneath. As offenses continue to move their best players inward, mainly to the slot positions, it is important for defenses to have an answer scheme wise. In running a match scheme, the safeties protect the inside third and allow the corners to play more of a man technique on the outside receiver.

--

By running a match scheme, and splitting the field, defensive coordinators can adjust to any offensive formation. This puts stress on an offense because the defense is not running blanket coverages, instead playing the best coverage for each particular formation. The match quarters concept is not revolutionary, or even new, but it does give defensive coordinators a flexible base to build a defense. The scheme itself is relatively easy to learn, and as long as a player can count to three they can run the scheme.

Cody Alexander

The How

Cody Alexander

All About the Cover Down

"In the construction of houses, choice of woods is made."

– Miyamoto Musashi, *The Book of Five Rings*

--

Understanding the structure of a defense is crucial in creating tactics that suppress offenses. How a defense chooses to align will have a direct effect on the plays that an offense chooses to attack it with.

--

Whether a defense is running a traditional 4-3 or a 4-2-5, how the defense chooses to create cover downs (alignments to the slots) will directly affect the way an offense chooses to attack the defense. Defending the spread successfully boils down to cover downs and over hangs. Over hangs are force players to the outside. In a Cover 3 scheme, the strong side outside linebacker (usually the Sam) and weak safety are the over hangs. In a traditional 4-3 or a two-high 4-2-5 scheme, the over hangs, or force players, are the Sam and the backside defensive end because the weak safety (boundary safety) is fit support and not primary support.

Regardless the base defense, utilizing cover downs are crucial to successfully defending the spread. Defensive coordinators that run a two-high shell must understand how their base defense dictates the plays the offense will run. The 4-3 is a more aggressive defense that relies on man coverage in the secondary. The 4-2-5 tries to eliminate RPOs by utilizing cover downs and uses the defensive ends as force players on the edge. This keeps the offense inside the box. One defense is built to stop the run while the other is built to defend the pass. Both are great defenses, but a coach must understand the structure of each in order to reach the defense's full potential.

--

The 4-3 Hybrid

In a traditional 4-3, the Sam is a box player and is primarily responsible for the run. Most 4-3s use the Sam as the outside force player to the strong side, making plays cutback to the Mike and Will. For the most part, when defenses run a 4-3, the Sam linebacker will still have a linebacker-type body with defensive coordinators opting for a thicker build to hold the edge.

Even though a "hybrid" player in most modern 4-3 schemes, the Sam is still primarily a run stopper and will fit the mold of a faster, more agile Will. Many defenses that face the spread on a regular basis will put the Sam to the field since he is technically the better coverage linebacker.

The biggest difference between a 4-3 scheme and its "smaller" offshoot, the 4-2-5, is the cover downs by the outside linebackers. Since the Sam is a box player in a 4-3, he is in an apex position, and squarely focused on the end man on the line of scrimmage (EMOL) acting as the primary force player to the strength. This alignment and assignment gives him a quick trigger on run support and allows the defense to gain a seven-man box against the run. Traditionally, the defensive ends in a 4-3 are in regular five techniques and read the offensive tackle in front of them. The aggressiveness of the linebackers in a 4-3 scheme allows more leeway for the defensive ends because the outside linebackers will correct their fits. An example of the 4-3 hybrid's run fits can be seen on the next page.

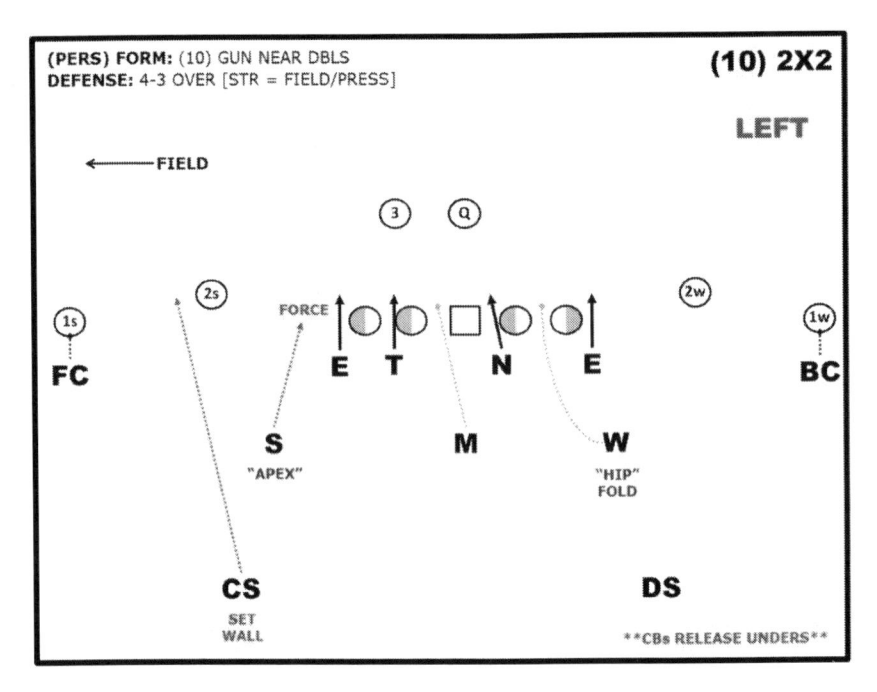

```
(PERS) FORM: (10) GUN NEAR DBLS                                    (10) 2X2
DEFENSE: 4-3 OVER [STR = FIELD/PRESS]
                                                                      LEFT
        ← FIELD

                              3      Q

              2s                                        2w
   1s                                                        1w
                  FORCE ↑  ○ ○  □  ○ ○ ↑
   FC                   E  T     N     E                     BC

                        S          M          W
                      "APEX"                "HIP"
                                            FOLD

                      CS                    DS
                      SET
                      WALL              **CBs RELEASE UNDERS**
```

The Sam's main objective in 4-3, even against the spread, is to be a force player on the edge, or fold into the box with a play away (cutback/reverse). He is working down towards the line of scrimmage against any run key, keeping his shoulders square, ready to drive on any handoff, keeping his outside arm free.

Against the pass, Sam is "cutting" to the hip of the #2 receiver and working to collision the route, assisting the safety as much as he can late. Teams that utilize a "true" Sam want to force the offense to throw the ball by bringing the outside linebackers quickly to fill their gaps and stuff the run, almost inviting an RPO or pass. The apex alignment of the Sam creates a sudden presence on the perimeter to the field and attempts to suffocate the offense's perimeter run game. The quick trigger of the Sam also allows the him to fold into the box and eliminate the cutback to the field when the play is away. Add the safeties to the fits with press quarters and technically a defense can achieve a nine-man box.

--

The lack of a cover down by the outside linebackers force the safeties in a quarters scheme to focus on the #2 WR in pseudo-man coverage. Unlike its sister in the 4-2-5, the 4-3 does not lend the safeties help in terms of an immediate buffer to a vertical route (cover down). Many teams that run a 4-3 utilize a press quarters scheme in the secondary. Press quarters coverage meshes well with the lack of provided cover down and the aggressive nature of the outside linebackers because it puts the secondary in semi-man coverage.

Press quarters coverage creates a man coverage blanket in the back end. On any pass read, the outside linebackers are flying to the near hips of the slot receivers ("cutting"), trying to collision them off their routes, and assist the slow bailing safeties. The pressing corners eliminate route combinations and force the offense to throw outside; low completion throws if they are going to attack the sideline vertically. Corners only release their man on any underneath route (drags/crossers). If the receiver runs a slant, the corner will top the route, compressing the receiver back to the line of scrimmage; all while getting eyes on #2. If #2 runs a corner route the coverage turns into Cloud and the corner and safety "cone" or vice the corner route with the safety holding the top.

Inside, the outside linebackers and the safeties are bracketing the slot receivers. The safeties essentially have them in man coverage with late help underneath. The pseudo-man coverage by the safeties allows the outside linebackers to be late support and aggressive to the run.

Against the run, the safeties will fit on the outside of the receiver, or correct the Sam if he bails too quickly from his run read. The lack of cover down puts pressure on the safeties to collision vertical routes and both safeties are susceptible to verticals off play-action. Another negative of press quarters from a 4-3 scheme is the lack of a push player against HBO concepts (fade/out). The safeties must drive on out cuts by the slot, exposing the intermediate zone and putting the safeties in a one-on-one open field-tackling situation with late support from the inside. Quarters coverage out of a 4-3 is susceptible to RPO teams because the outside linebackers are quick to fill on run keys leaving the secondary in one-on-one situations across the board. One way to combat this is to run Cloud (see next page).

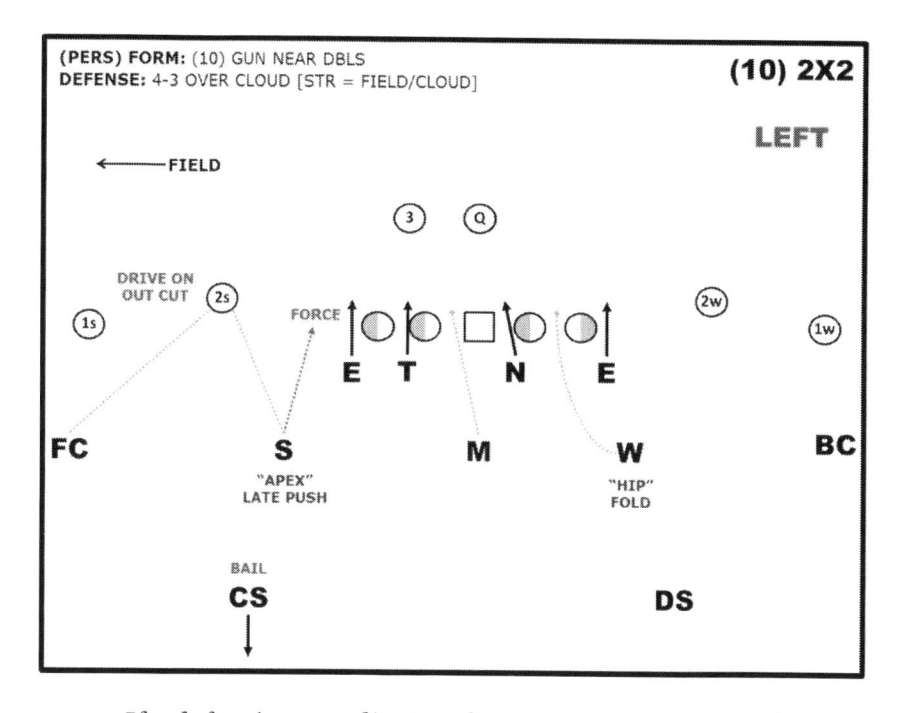

```
(PERS) FORM: (10) GUN NEAR DBLS
DEFENSE: 4-3 OVER CLOUD [STR = FIELD/CLOUD]                    (10) 2X2

                                                                LEFT
        ←——FIELD

                              ③    ⓠ

         DRIVE ON
         OUT CUT  (2s)
   (1s)           FORCE ↑○↑○ □ ○↑○↑        (2w)
                        E  T  N  E                    (1w)

   FC              S           M           W           BC
                "APEX"                   "HIP"
              LATE PUSH                   FOLD

                   BAIL
                   CS                      DS
                   ↓
```

If a defensive coordinator chooses to run a Cloud scheme, as shown above, to complement the 4-3 and to combat RPOs, the outside linebackers have the luxury to "hang" in their position and be late to push when a pass read is given. As stated earlier, one of the negatives of the 4-3 quarters scheme is its susceptibility to HBO concepts or now screens off RPOs or play-action (bubble/switch). A natural way to alleviate the pressure put on the outside linebackers to fill quickly, yet be of help in the pass, is to run a Cloud concept.

Once offenses identify that a team is running a quarters scheme, and the outside linebackers are filling fast, it is a natural reaction for the offense to start throwing push routes towards the boundaries. The Cloud concept is a great change-up to press quarters and can even function as a base coverage. The luxury in a Cloud concept comes from the corners driving on any out cut by the #2 receiver. The safety holds the top of the coverage, which is a negative to press quarters where safeties are exposed to vertical routes. At least with a Cloud concept, the defense can protect itself deep while having an answer to underneath routes. The "trap" corners also help with any RPO screen and the bailing safeties give third-level RPO teams a run read into aggressive linebackers.

--

The Single-Gap 4-2-5

The 4-2-5 evolved because offenses were putting more receivers on the field. A dilemma on how a defense should play the slot receivers and protect the hybrid player, or Sam linebacker, soon followed. Initially, defenses set the Sam to the passing strength, but as spread offenses have evolved, and added tempo, defensive coordinators are going back to setting the Sam to the field and leaving him there.

The point of a 4-2-5 is to gain a cover down on the slot receiver to the field, or the most dangerous person in space. The defensive line, or front, is set to protect the hybrid player and allow for maximum cover down. The difference in philosophy for a 4-2-5 teams is how aggressive the Sam is in the run game.

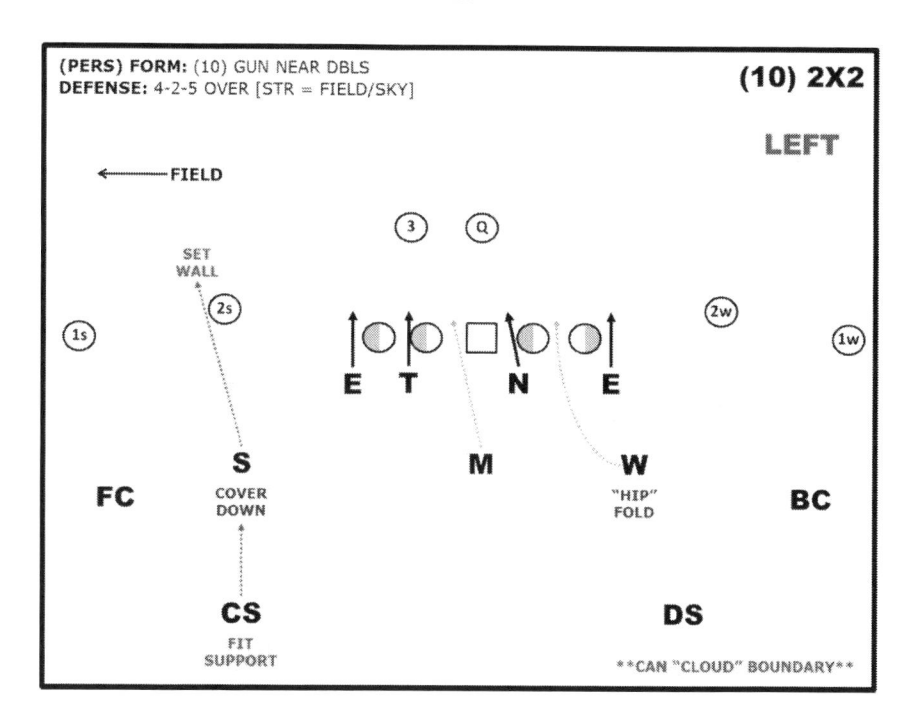

--

```
(PERS) FORM: (10) GUN NEAR DBLS                           (10) 2X2
DEFENSE: 4-2-5 OVER [STR = FIELD/SKY]
                                                          LEFT
         ← FIELD
                              ③    ⓠ
              SET
              WALL
               ↑
              (2s)                              (2w)
    (1s)      |O|O|□|O|O|                                 (1w)
              E  T  N  E
              S           M           W
    FC      COVER                    "HIP"        BC
            DOWN                     FOLD
              ↑
              CS                      DS
              FIT
              SUPPORT                **CAN "CLOUD" BOUNDARY**
```

In a quarters scheme, the outside linebackers work with the safeties to bracket the slot receivers. Modern spread teams are moving their best athletes inside if not putting them at QB. This allows the offense to move their best athlete around (motions) and get him involved in the run game while maximizing his position in the middle of the field for high percentage throws. As defensive coordinators have begun to learn spread tendencies, many teams are opting to move to a **Sky Press** scheme.

Much like the press scheme utilized by 4-3 teams, the 4-2-5 defenses create added benefit with a full cover down. The Sam in a 4-2-5 is not a box player. The only linebackers involved in the box are the fitters (Mike and Will). This added player in the secondary creates extra help on the offense's most dangerous player, the slot. The Sam and safety work together to high-low bracket the slot. In match quarters, the Sam does not leave the slot unless someone crosses his face. This gives the safety much needed vertical support, something that might not happen in a 4-3 apex scheme.

Against the run, the outside linebacker to the strength creates cutbacks by fitting on the outside of the slot receivers. Unlike the 4-3 where the outside linebacker to the strength is the primary force player, in the 4-2-5 the defensive end accepts that role. The wall support of the outside linebacker along with the force of the defensive end creates a tunnel for the safety. The cover down by the strong side outside linebackers allows the safety to be slow off the line and fit inside the slot. This vice action gives the defense a maximum chance of making a tackle or forcing the runner into an unblocked defender. Many defensive coordinators set the three technique (Over Front) to the field regardless of where the back aligns to gain maximum cover down and put an extra lineman to the field. The Will (fold player) is the conflicted player because he must attack a gap (boundary "B") while relating to the slot against the pass.

Like in a 4-3 hybrid scheme, the biggest negative for quarters is the out cuts by the slot. In a 4-2-5, the Sam's full cover down to the field limits exposure to an out cut. The Sam's alignment allows him to get his hands on the slot and break to the top shoulder of an out route. Just because the Sam is covered down to the slot does not mean he is not aggressive to the run. He is a wall builder to the outside of the slot allowing the safety to attack downhill instead of running the alley.

On any run, the Sam is attacking the slot and working to cross his face, creating a cutback. The defensive ends in many quarters schemes align tight to the tackles and create natural gap exchanges. These exchanges allow for the wide cover down of the Sam. If a defensive end has a Nose, he can go inside to the "B" gap on any out block ("heavy" technique), and the outside linebacker to that side fits the outside gap ("hang" technique). The benefit of the safeties in the fits is the reason why many teams are opting to go away from the traditional 4-2-5 "Blue" or Cloud coverage made famous by TCU's Gary Patterson (image on next page). In Cloud, the safeties are fast bailing to top the any vertical to their side.

This technique makes them secondary support and takes them out of the run fit.

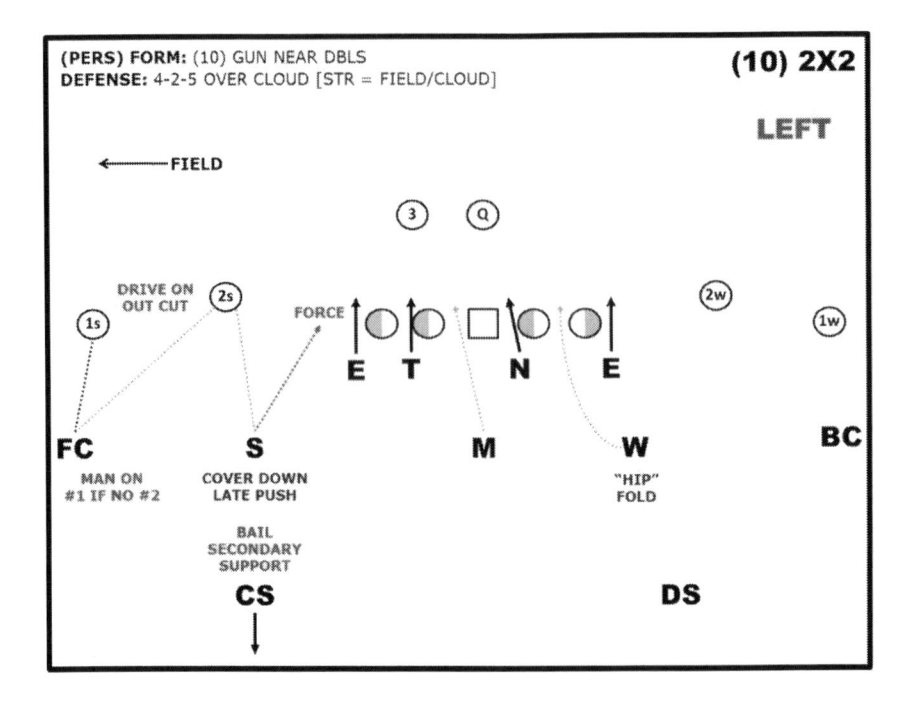

```
(PERS) FORM: (10) GUN NEAR DBLS                          (10) 2X2
DEFENSE: 4-2-5 OVER CLOUD [STR = FIELD/CLOUD]
                                                            LEFT
        ←——— FIELD

                              ③     ⓠ

            DRIVE ON  ②ₛ
            OUT CUT           FORCE↑
    ①ₛ                                              ②w
                        ⭕ ◐  ☐ ◐ ◐|                       ①w
                        E  T    N  E

    FC          S              M        W                 BC
    MAN ON    COVER DOWN              "HIP"
    #1 IF NO #2  LATE PUSH            FOLD

              BAIL
            SECONDARY
             SUPPORT
              CS                            DS
              ↓
```

Most defensive coordinators start building a defensive scheme by defending the run first. For that reason, Cloud coverage has evolved to fit alongside the 4-2-5. The outside support of the corners allow the outside linebackers to be patient and aggressively attack the line of scrimmage when the ball is handed off. The biggest difference between the ultra-aggressiveness of the 4-3 (apex the Sam to gain quicker force) and the 4-2-5 (maximize the cover down) is how the players to the field interact with each other.

The most famous of the 4-2-5 coverages, TCU's "Blue" coverage (think Cloud/Two-Read) allows the Sam to maximize his run fit from a covered down position. If the Sam is quick to fit the run, he is susceptible to RPOs and out cuts by the slot. To combat this, Cloud coverage was meshed with the full cover down seen in most 4-2-5s. The Sam and Will in a Cloud concept can hold their position ("hang") and expand with the pass once they have read their keys.

Against the run, the Sam can start moving towards the edge of the box, yet still be protected because he has the curl and does not need to push with an out cut by the slot. In TCU's defense, the defensive ends play "wide fives" and attack the edges of the box (force players), forcing everything back for the box linebackers (Mike and Will). The wide fives act as natural barriers for offenses trying to work the ball outside. Combine the wide fives with Cloud coverage and the "hanging" outside linebackers act as extra support if anything leaks, making the defensive ends right.

--

Cover downs, in general, allow the safeties to be ultra-aggressive because they are relying on the outside linebackers to get their hands on the slots as soon as the ball is snapped, slowing the receivers' vertical releases. This ultra-aggressiveness in quarters is where defense can be exposed to big plays in the middle of the field if the safety does not hold is line. A way to neutralize this threat is to run a Cloud concept in the back end, keeping the safeties deep and out of fit support.

    The wide cover downs of a 4-2-5 can adversely affect the run fits if the Sam and safety get too far from the box. Against teams like Baylor, under former head coach Art Briles, who line their outside receivers outside the numbers, teams have designed built in split rules to offset the open space.

    Split rules change the coverage depending on the splits of the receivers. It would not make sense for a Sam to widen his cover down all the way to the numbers, or a safety to run Cloud when the receivers are spread too far apart for him to reach a vertical by #1. Each coverages is predicated on where the recievers line up in relation to each other and the offensive line. Stack and the coverage turns into Cloud. If the receivers line up in a traditional alignment or far apart, the safeties check to Sky. Coverages can also be dependent on down and distance.

    The ability to change coverages depending on the splits is a unique adaptation of split field coverage and modern 4-2-5 schemes. Splitting the secondary in half allows defenses to call the right coverages dependent on what the defense is seeing on either side of the ball.

--

4-3 hybrid or 4-2-5, it really boils down to preference and the athletes in a program. Each defense has its positives and negatives. The style should reflect the defensive coordinator's comfort level and the offenses seen on a regular basis. The 4-3 apex style lends itself to run heavy offenses, but defenses must be aware of the RPO and the one-on-one matchup of the safety. In a pass heavy district/conference the 4-2-5 is a great place to start. The goal versus the spread is to have a plus one in the run as well as the pass. The 4-3/4-2-5 defenses allow a defensive coordinator to keep a two-high shell and attack the box at the same time.

Cody Alexander

Designing a Modern Defense

"Simplicity is the ultimate sophistication." — Leonardo da Vinci

--

As tempo becomes more ingrained in modern football, it is important for defensive coordinators to design schemes that are simple to learn yet sophisticated enough to keep offenses on their toes. Flexible and adaptive. Two foundational principles of a split field quarters defense.

--

Defense is a science; it has its own rules and theories. These rules allow each individual player on the field to line up in the correct position and attack the offense in an organized and structured fashion. The theories are the play calls and alignments, each one playing off the tendencies of an offense. The defense is always reactionary, even when acting as the aggressor. Any great defensive coach knows that changing the way an offense attacks a defense is key in winning games; make the offense left handed. In order for a defense to do its job, it has to change what the offense is trying to do.

The best way to change an offense's structure is to use pressures and blitzes to attack its schemes. Each pressure in a defensive scheme is designed to defeat an offensive tendency, whether it is a run blitz or fire zone. The key with any pressure is to make sure it aligns correctly to the offensive formation and is sound against the run and pass. In the past, defensive coordinators were concerned with field and boundary when blitzing, ignoring where the formation strength was located.

Football is evolving every year. The spread offense is dominating the football landscape and challenging how defensive coordinators call their defenses. The extra pressure of tempo causes some defensive coaches to panic. Offenses are reading the alignment of the defense pre-snap and attacking it on simple reads at a devastating rate. It is hard for a defensive coach not to press and get ultra-aggressive, or worse, passive (static). Calling pressures are easy. Most blitzes, or pressures, are designed to defeat specific offensive plays, protections, or formations, but with offenses being fluid with personnel and tempo, it can become a guessing game.

Modern defensive coaches must approach game planning with a different train of thought than their former counterparts. Formations, above all else, have to be in the forefront of a defensive coach's analysis. When designing a base defense, the first thing a defensive coordinator must do is define how the defense will align against an offense's base formations. This is important in not only getting the defense in the right alignment but also helping defensive players learn the intricacies of football.

Formationing defensive calls allow the defensive coordinator to eliminate wordy play calls and get the call out to the players who are seeing the formation in real time. Need an edge pressure that sends a rusher to back's side? Call it, and the Mike reads the formation, signals to the blitzing linebacker, and tells the front the movement all in seconds. This allows the defense to match the offense. The modern spread offense packages plays together to get the best play call versus the defensive alignment. Defenses can do this too through alignment and blitzing the formation, not strong/weak or field/boundary.

--

Every defensive play call is a check, and every call has "autos" and "Omahas" (get out of the call and check back to the base defense). Each blitz created has an optimum way of running it. Modern spread defenses need to have checks that allow the defense to adjust and keep its base rules. Here is an example, if a defense is running a fire zone that sends the Sam and Mike off the edge, it works great against any 2x2 or 2x1 set, but if the offense aligns in a Trips formation the Sam's cover down is compromised.

Compromised Sam – Will must sling to #3:

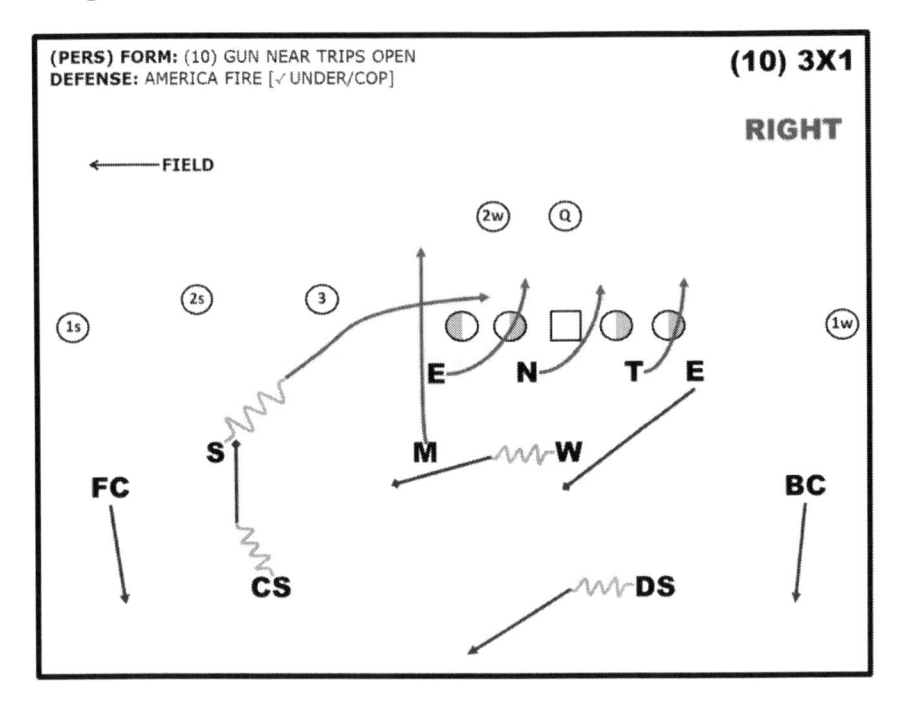

(PERS) FORM: (10) GUN NEAR TRIPS OPEN
DEFENSE: AMERICA FIRE [✓ UNDER/COP]

(10) 3X1

RIGHT

Instead of being able to hide the blitz, the Sam now has to work from the #2 receiver and attack the edge. This also does not mention the Will needing to sling to the #3 receiver, all the way from the boundary. On paper, the blitz works, but in real time it makes no sense. If a defense were able to check the blitz, the Sam would cover down on #2; the safety would spin down on #3 and the Mike and Will would run the blitz (see next page).

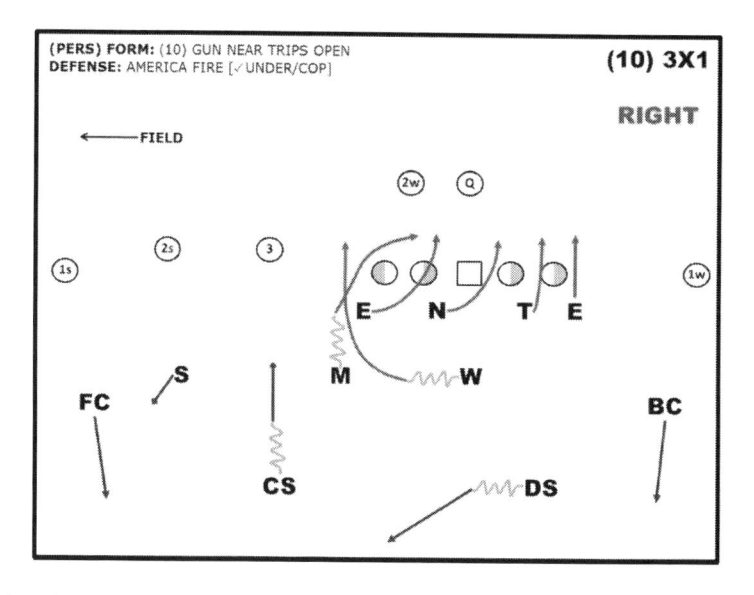

(PERS) FORM: (10) GUN NEAR TRIPS OPEN
DEFENSE: AMERICA FIRE [✓ UNDER/COP]

(10) 3X1

RIGHT

Taking it one step further, if the blitz was by formation and the rule was to blitz the back, the wrapper would always be to the back's side and able to peel if the back flared. This would be ideal, rather a linebacker defending a back than a defensive end, and in the case of Gun Far, the Down Safety (see below).

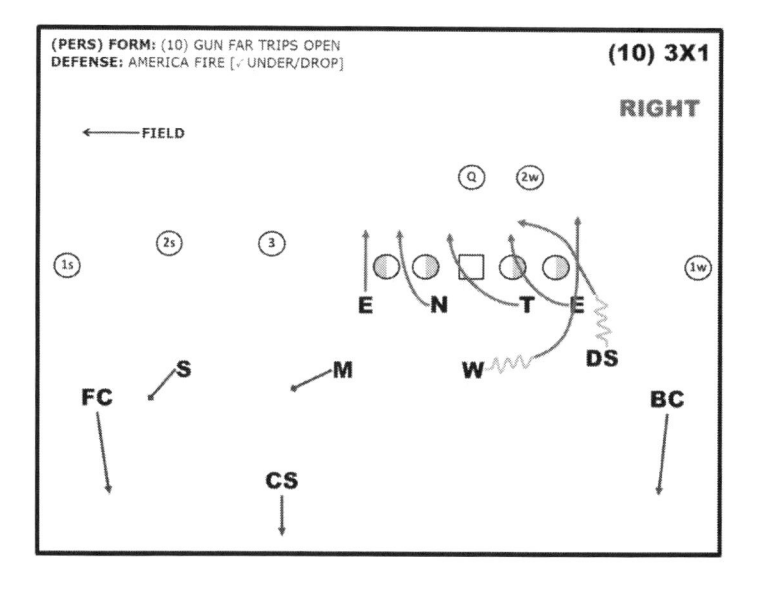

(PERS) FORM: (10) GUN FAR TRIPS OPEN
DEFENSE: AMERICA FIRE [✓ UNDER/DROP]

(10) 3X1

RIGHT

- 103 -

This adjustment allows the modern defense to keep its principles. Against motion, rigid defenses either stick with the blitz or "Omaha," getting out of it completely. If a defensive coordinator "Omahas" out of blitzes against motion, then an offense is going to motion to keep the defense in its base (static = predictable).

It is important to have a plan when designing pressures. Not every blitz is going to work versus every formation. A defensive coordinator must have checks within the actual call. Packaging blitzes from the same tree together like the one illustrated on the prior page, eliminates the guessing game of how the offense will align and whether the call is good to the boundary or field. Packaging blitzes by blitz tree permits the formation to be the indicator, consequently, a defense is always in the right call.

Bill Belichick and Buddy Ryan have made "Blitzing to Formation" famous. Each blitz has a check system predicated on offensive alignment. This allows the defensive coordinator to make one call and stick with it. For example, a defensive coordinator calls an edge blitz with full line movement and has a rule that the blitz always comes from the side of the back. Building checks with in pressures allows the defensive players to know how to align and where to send the defensive linemen every time, regardless of the formation. If the offense uses a tight end, the call will go to the open-side. Whether the set is 2x2 or 3x1, there is a check for that.

--

With offenses creating new ways to package plays, it makes sense for a defense to do the same. A defensive call sheet should be limited against spread teams and even smaller against those that utilize tempo. This is not a reduction in pressures; just packaging them in a way that allows the defense to react quickly. If a defensive coordinator is guessing, most likely the offense will catch up.

Streamlining or packaging pressures allows the defensive coordinator to react quickly and cleaner to each situation. Even simple line movements and single-dog (one linebacker) pressures can be packaged together. Knowledge is power. All coaches know this. Verbiage gets in the way of many players being successful because they have to remember too much. Eliminate the verbiage by packaging calls from the same tree. Offenses have proven over time that simple is not only better but also explosive. So why not follow suit and beat them at their own game?

Cody Alexander

Setting the Strength

"There are no absolute rules of conduct, either in peace or war. Everything depends on circumstances." – Leon Trotsky

--

How a defense decides to set its strength is one of the most import decisions a defensive coordinator will make when designing a defense. Modern offenses push defensive tactics to the limit. A coordinator must understand the foundational principles of the modern spread offense in order to combat it. Football has become an intellectuals game.

--

Every defense has a strength call. Depending on how a defensive coordinator decides to set the strength can determine if a defense is more susceptible to motions/shifts and formations into the boundary (FIB), which will be discussed in the next chapter. The strength call sets the defense's anchor points and dictates everything from run fits to pass distribution. Making the right strength call can be the difference between a tackle for a loss or giving up a touchdown. Regardless of how a defense sets the strength, it is important that everything stem from the strength call, blitzing to coverage.

A defense's base needs to have sound, fundamental rules that are easy for players to learn and allows them to react quickly to the offense's formation. Building a defense that recognizes formations and adjusts to them is the best way to approach setting the strength. There are two main theories when it comes to setting the strength, *strong/weak* or *field/boundary*.

--

Strong/Weak

In a traditional 4-3/3-4 the strength will be set to the offense's strength, which traditionally has been determined by a tight end or the passing strength (2x2 = strength to the back – 20 personnel and 3x1 = strength to the most receiver side). If the defense is setting the strength strong/weak the offense can take advantage of this in an 11 personnel set.

By putting the tight end on the line, the offense is forcing the defense to set the strength to the extra gap. In a traditional 4-3 defense, the Sam linebacker is usually the most athletic of the three, and as more teams turn to the spread, the Sam is becoming a hybrid Nickel defender (a safety playing near the box). If the defense is setting the strength to the tight end, the offense can ensure the Sam aligns in the box, and the Will isolated on receivers. Using a traditional strong/weak call can be a good adjustment to power teams that base primarily in 21 personnel formations. The issue with setting the front by strength is really glaring when facing modern spread teams.

Versus spread teams, the offense can use the strong/weak call against the defense much easier. As more offenses began running the spread, defensive coordinators started to align the defense by passing strength. Instead of going to the tight end the Sam now went to the most receiver side. Though the Sam was in a better position, the defense was still vulnerable to motions and shifts.

Teams that run the spread can force the Sam into the boundary and isolate the Will to the field. Once a team has set the strength into the boundary, all the offense has to do is motion back to the field, and now the defense has to flip. The worst thing a defense can do is flip players' alignments mid-snap. Change of strength motion can bring havoc to teams that call the strength by strong/weak. With one simple across-field motion, the defense is now out leveraged and out of alignment.

Defenses that call the strength this way are trying to keep the Sam out of the box, but leave themselves vulnerable to motions and shifts. Even if a defense sets the Sam to the passing strength, the offense can set the formation into the boundary and motion back to the field ensuring the Sam and Will are out of position and overmatched.

--

Field/Boundary

The modern age of spread has forced defensive coordinators everywhere to rethink their approach; even down to the basics of setting the strength. It is amazing how cyclical football can be. With the advent of spread football, one of the oldest forms of defense, the 4-3 Over Front is now the new in vogue defense. Not everything old is good; things have to change as the parameters of the game change. Modern defenses must make adjustments in order to stay up with an offense-centric game. As tempo becomes more a part of the game, and as more teams get better at doing it, the best way to stay clean is to call the strength by field/boundary and divorce the front from the secondary.

Setting the strength by field/boundary lends itself to the split field quarters scheme many teams are turning to when combating the up-tempo spread attacks that are proliferating through football. A split field defense should set the Sam to the field and the Will to the boundary. The theory behind this is simple, put the defense's best athletes in space to mirror the spread, setting the lesser athletes, and box linebacker, to the boundary where the offense cannot attack them with space. The only exception is the corner position; teams should set their best man coverage corner to the boundary and their best zone corner to the field. By leaving the Sam to the field, a defense is much quicker to line up. This does not change how defenses set the front. The front should be divorced from the secondary call and predicated on the formation in a field/boundary defense.

When facing tempo teams it is easy for players to align the right way when all they have to identify is where the hash is. A majority of the game is played on a hash, so it is important for a defensive coach to consider this. In addition, players learn to relate off each other and become solid units. If running a split field scheme, a defense can have two completely separate units that work in tandem together, Mike being the go-between.

In a field/boundary concept, the corner, safety, and outside linebacker all work together, all the time. Running a split field scheme allows the same players to work off each other over the course of a season and allows teammates to quickly asses if someone is out of alignment. By keeping players together as mini-units, they can help each other align and see landmarks quicker.

The major issue with calling the strength this by field/boundary is the Sam linebacker. In a typical single-gap 4-2-5 the Sam is the hybrid player and must be protected from the box to allow full cover downs. Teams turn to the 4-2-5 or 3-4 Okie hybrids to get an extra athlete on the field against spread teams and use their defensive ends to create natural walls around the box.

In modern football, with the spread dominating every level, the Sam has become the key link between the secondary and the front seven. The issue with the Sam arises when teams put the formation into the boundary. When setting the strength by field/boundary an offense can set the Trips formation into the boundary and make the Sam the new "Mike." This situation for many coordinators is not a desirable option, but if a defense plays on the law of averages, the offense is not going to run a formation into the boundary like Trips and Trey (TE Trips) the entire game. In fact, a defensive coordinator could argue that by setting the strength this way a defense is forcing the offense to be "left-handed" and into less space. The opposite of what a spread offense wants. 3x1 formations are the only sets that make the Sam a

"Mike" linebacker and bring him directly into the middle of the box. In 20 personnel, the Sam can become the Will, which is a much easier transition than to hold the middle of the box versus Trips, especially if the defense utilizes gap exchanges in their fits.

--

Here are five points of emphasis when setting the strength:

1. If a defense is seeing a lot of tempo, it is probably best to set the strength by field and boundary. In the middle of field, the Sam will always go to the running back's side in 2x2 and the passing strength in every other set.
2. Setting the strength by strong/weak, or putting the Sam to the passing strength no matter if the formation is to the boundary, can leave a defense susceptible to motions. Any change of strength motion will essentially put the Will linebacker into coverage and bring the Sam back into the box. By leaving the Sam to the field, the defense has forced the offense to use less space to attack the weakness in its scheme.
3. The only issue with setting the strength by field/boundary is when teams run Trips sets into the boundary (FIB). If the Sam is an extra safety, this can be an issue. For most 4-

2-5 defenses, the Sam is a hybrid and built to withstand a few plays in the box. If a defense knows a team will try and FIB the defense it may want to work the Sam in the box a few times during practice.

4. If teams are using FIB to get the Sam in the box, the defense can use line movement and pressures to alleviate the hybrid Sam. Edge blitzes from the weak side versus 20 personnel can get the Sam out of the box versus FIB and set the front to the two-receiver side to align the Sam in the "B" gap and get a natural exchange with the field defensive end versus zone away.

5. With anything, there is a choice, a coordinator must make sure how he sets the strength aligns with his overall philosophy. If a defense does not see many spread and tempo teams, it may be beneficial to set the front by strong/weak rules. Tempo and spread force the defense to simplify, and one quick and easy way to set the defense up is to align the strength by field/boundary.

Defending Formations into the Boundary

"Never attempt to win by force what can be won by deception."
— Niccolò Machiavelli, *The Prince*

--

The offense uses formation into the boundary to deceive the defense into thinking it has them cornered. Defensive coordinators must treat FIB differently than if the same formation is was aligned in the field.

--

Putting the offense's fastest players or aligning a formation's strength into the boundary may seem like an illogical thing to do considering spread teams value space. Many times, offenses are aligning into the boundary because of how defenses react. Offenses use formation into the boundary (FIB) for several purposes: 1) to get the defense to over rotated and expose the field; 2) to take advantage of how the defense sets its strength; or 3) to isolate the offense's receiving threat to the field (most likely in single coverage).

Defenses struggle with FIB because they cannot align to these formations the same way as if they were to the field. If a defense does not adjust to the offense's reduced set, or tries to spin into the boundary, the offense can quickly out leverage the defense with shifts/motions, or by running a stretch/speed opting to the field. The pressure put on the defense in a single-receiver set (3x1/2x1) is even greater when the formation is to the boundary. In these formations, the offense can create a one-on-one matchup with the cornerback and their number one receiving threat to the field with ample space.

Most offenses are not patient enough to play their whole game into the boundary. By setting the formation strength into the boundary, the offense is reducing the field of play, contradicting a main principle within the spread offense. Very rarely, an offense will run a 3x1 formation into the boundary and run four vertical routes. Defenses can use this to their advantage when designing ways to attack FIBs.

Offenses use FIB to run switch/rub routes, high-low concepts, and isolate the field defenders (run or pass). In order to combat an offense's FIB plays, the defense must have a plan that protects the leverage to the field but does not give up numbers to the boundary. Staying two-high and splitting the coverage gives the defense an advantage. The isolation pass in single-receiver formations is still there, but only on a low completion percentage fade route. The corner and safety to the field must communicate and be aware of the situation. Sky coverage can be utilized to protect the underneath of the post route coming into the field while using the safety as a plus one defender against any run. The defense should shy away from using press on either side of the formation and force the offense to throw fades to the field or block in limited space to the boundary.

--

10 Personnel 2x2

The way offenses attack the defense in 10 personnel is by creating a "3 into" situation for the defense. In a 2x2 formation, the offense is forcing the Mike to open to the boundary versus pass, which reduces the numbers to the field. Even against the run, the Mike has to hold the field side "A" gap if the defense is setting the front to the field. If the front is set to the back, the Sam is now in conflict from depth (field side), leaving the field safety (CS) in a one-on-one situation to the field versus play-action. Teams that set the running back into the boundary versus a defense that sets the three technique to the back will flip their RPO read and force the Sam to fold into the "B" gap. Again, this creates a one-on-one situation with the safety, this time an open-field tackle. The main objective for setting the strength to the field is to eliminate the one-on-one situations in space. The offense has already forfeited the luxury of space aligning the formation into the boundary and it is the defense's job to use the sideline to its advantage.

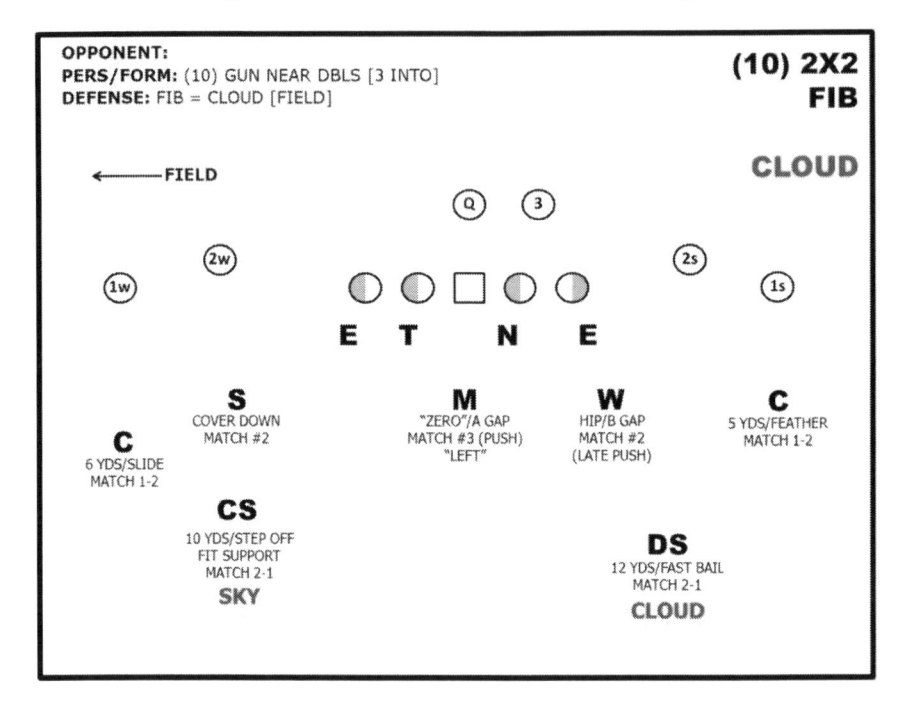

```
OPPONENT:
PERS/FORM: (10) GUN NEAR DBLS [3 INTO]              (10) 2X2
DEFENSE: FIB = CLOUD [FIELD]                            FIB

        ←—— FIELD                                    CLOUD

                            Q    3

            2w                                  2s
     1w          ◐  ◐  □  ◐  ◐                      1s
                 E  T  N  E

              S            M           W           C
          COVER DOWN   "ZERO"/A GAP  HIP/B GAP  5 YDS/FEATHER
   C       MATCH #2   MATCH #3 (PUSH) MATCH #2   MATCH 1-2
6 YDS/SLIDE             "LEFT"    (LATE PUSH)
 MATCH 1-2
              CS
          10 YDS/STEP OFF              DS
           FIT SUPPORT             12 YDS/FAST BAIL
            MATCH 2-1                MATCH 2-1
              SKY                     CLOUD
```

The best way to handle a 2x2 "3 Into" situation is to set the front to the field and run a Cloud scheme to the boundary (above). Running a split-field scheme gives the defense an advantage over the offense because it can now dictate the fits on either side of the formation. Many offenses will align in a FIB set to run switch routes or high-low concepts. Running Cloud to the boundary sets the defense up to combat any high-low scheme or vertical switch route. Cloud coverage also enables the Will to hold his position on the hip of the defensive end and allows him to attack his open gap versus a run. The natural vantage point of the corner in Cloud allows for smooth transitions if the receivers run vertical switch routes.

Teams that like to RPO into the boundary with receiver screens are dealt with when running Cloud to the boundary. The corner is quick to attack the screen, and the Will can be secondary support from the inside once the ball is thrown.

To the field, the Sam is able to gain a full cover down on the slot essentially eliminating any threat of a cross-read RPO (read the linebacker opposite the back). Setting the three technique to the field also creates a solid wall against the run and allows the field defensive end to hold his position if the offense runs a power read, boxing everything back to the short side.

--

10 personnel Trips

Trips into the boundary stresses the defense to the max. Many offenses will use Trips formations into the boundary to force the defense to rotate its defenders into a confined space. If the defense does not adjust, the offense has a numbers advantage and can build a wall for receiver screens.

To the field, the 3x1 set creates a one-on-one situation with the corner and the "X" receiver. Most offenses will not run a four vertical scheme with Trips into; there just is not enough space. To combat receiver screens, a defensive coordinator may choose to spin to a Cover 3 look to maximize the box numbers and cover down to the Trips side. This tendency has the ability to backfire on a defense. By rotating to the Trips side, the defense is leaving the five technique as the last man standing against the stretch. Teams also like to run Power Read and jet motion from Trips into because defenses have a tendency to over rotate to the Trips side. The key versus Trips into is to stay even and protect the field.

With three receivers in such a tight window, the defense can play on the law of averages that the offense is not going to run four vertical, and if they do, the boundary corner can cover the #1 and #2 receiver by himself with the Will underneath. The best coverage for Trips into is Stress (see next page).

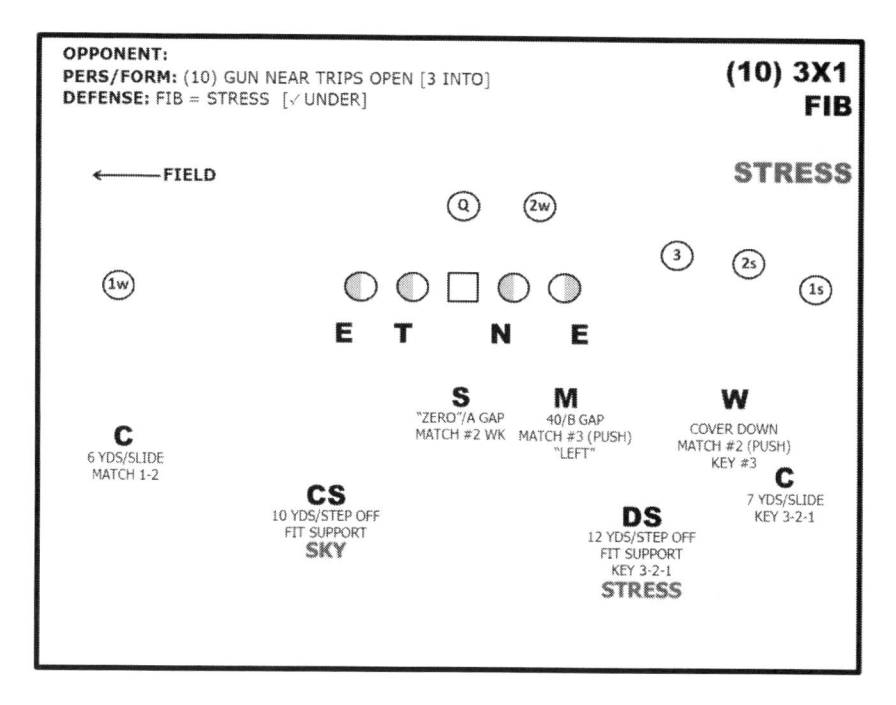

```
OPPONENT:
PERS/FORM: (10) GUN NEAR TRIPS OPEN [3 INTO]              (10) 3X1
DEFENSE: FIB = STRESS  [✓ UNDER]                               FIB

←——FIELD                                                    STRESS

                         Q     2w
                                              3      2s
      1w         ●  ●  □  ●  ●                              1s
                 E   T   N   E

                         S        M         W
                      "ZERO"/A GAP  40/B GAP   COVER DOWN
         C            MATCH #2 WK  MATCH #3 (PUSH)  MATCH #2 (PUSH)
      6 YDS/SLIDE                  "LEFT"      KEY #3
      MATCH 1-2         CS                                  C
                    10 YDS/STEP OFF    DS              7 YDS/SLIDE
                    FIT SUPPORT    12 YDS/STEP OFF    KEY 3-2-1
                       SKY         FIT SUPPORT
                                   KEY 3-2-1
                                     STRESS
```

Stress allows the Will to maximize his cover down and set a wall against any screen. The Will's main objective versus a receiver screen is to cross the face of the slot and turn everything back into the field. Since the boundary safety is essentially playing Sky coverage from a deeper alignment, he can be aggressive to the screen as long as the #3 receiver does not go vertical. The corner can plant and drive on the screen with ball thrown.

The Mike's alignment is a "40" because the luxury of little space allows him to be tight to the box. Since he is matching the #3 receiver, he can hold his alignment and still reach his man versus any vertical. Against RPO teams, running an Under Front to Trips allows the Mike to hold his alignment even more, taking the quarterback if he pulls on a Zone Read or flying to the screen with ball thrown.

The only negative to aligning the back seven of the defense by field boundary, as shown on the previous page, is putting the Sam at the Mike versus Trips FIB. The reasoning for aligning the Sam to the field is to combat across-field motions. If the defense sets the Sam to the passing strength, the offense can align with Trips into and motion back to the field, isolating the Will in space. This was discussed in the previous chapter.

The field safety has to be the adjuster in the run game and his role is the fit player. Against the run, the field safety will attack the "O" gap. If the offense runs a power read, the field safety can correct the fits of the Sam and defensive end to buy time for the other players to get out from the boundary, most likely fitting outside the pulling guard

Stress coverage allows the defense to sit back without being passive. Running Sky to the field creates a "robber" concept to eliminate slant/post routes. The field corner treats the single receiver with man principles, all along understanding he will have help late and underneath (this is why he will not play press – eliminate quick throws). The key versus any FIB set is not pressing the corner if the receiver is by himself (to the field) or outside the numbers (to the boundary). Pressing allows the offense to have a quick hitting throw to the field, and can eliminate the corner from fitting to the boundary. As stated earlier, the key cog in the whole scheme is the field safety. His role is crucial in eliminating the run, and robbing the underneath throws to a locked corner.

--

11 Personnel

Many coaches do not realize the issues that arise when an offense sets the tight end and the running back into the boundary in Pro Twin. The issues created in 10 personnel 2x2 are mirrored in its 11 personnel counterpart. Offenses set the back into the boundary to create cover down issues to the field. Many defenses adjust to Pro Twin by bumping the linebackers over a gap (Will in the "C" and Mike in the "A") and have the Sam fold into the open "B" gap (this scheme is called "Squeeze"). Against RPO teams, it is easy to get a cross-read on an RPO (read the conflict player away from the back). With the extra gap created by the tight end, the defense must account for it and most do using their linebackers.

The more efficient way to attack the Pro Twin FIB is to run a "Cheat" alignment (see next page). This scheme forces the offense into the boundary. The three-on-two to the field and the illusion of an open "C" gap to the boundary make it more enticing for the offense to attack the boundary. By forcing the offense into the boundary, and embracing FIB formations, the defense is shrinking the field and giving the defense back the advantage.

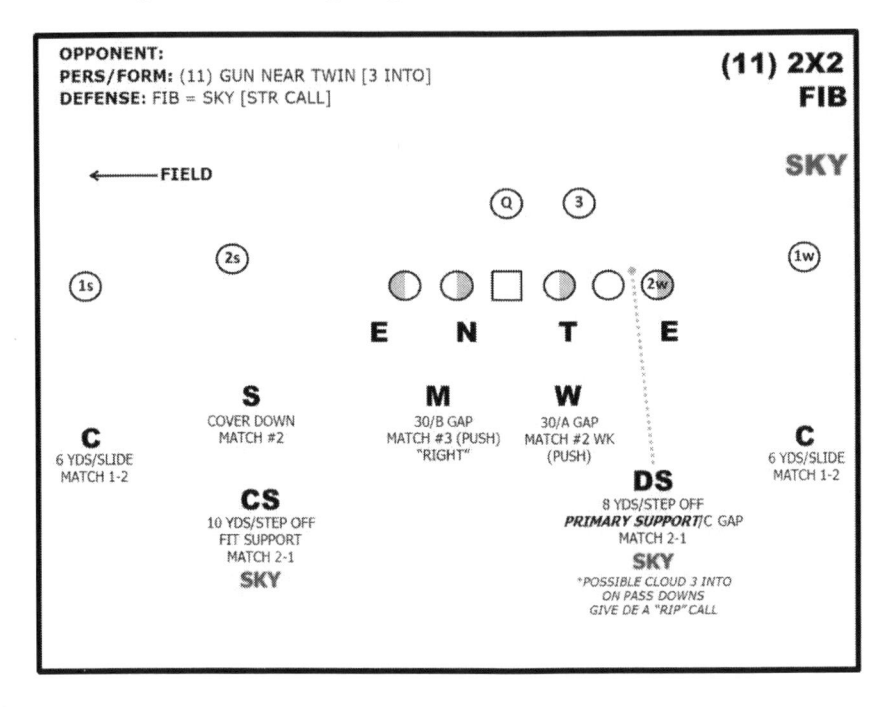

```
OPPONENT:                                               (11) 2X2
PERS/FORM: (11) GUN NEAR TWIN [3 INTO]                      FIB
DEFENSE: FIB = SKY [STR CALL]

    ←——FIELD                                             SKY

                            Q    3

             2s                                         1w
     1s              O  O  □  O  O 2w
                        E  N  T  E

            S
     C    COVER DOWN   M           W                      C
  6 YDS/SLIDE MATCH #2  30/B GAP    30/A GAP           6 YDS/SLIDE
   MATCH 1-2          MATCH #3 (PUSH) MATCH #2 WK       MATCH 1-2
                       "RIGHT"       (PUSH)
                                                   DS
            CS                                 8 YDS/STEP OFF
      10 YDS/STEP OFF                        PRIMARY SUPPORT/C GAP
       FIT SUPPORT                               MATCH 2-1
        MATCH 2-1                                  SKY
          SKY                              *POSSIBLE CLOUD 3 INTO
                                              ON PASS DOWNS
                                           GIVE DE A "RIP" CALL
```

The boundary safety plays a "robber" technique and is in primary run support (responsible for a gap) because he is involved in the box fit. Inside the box, the Mike and Will align in 30s. This gives the Will a better angle to defend the pass, and the Mike is in a perfect position to attack flow either way. The Sam is able to cover down to the slot, eliminating any cross-read RPO. The field safety can now focus on the two receivers to his side, fitting off the

Sam. Many times teams try to run a pick/flat combination or a high-low scheme into the boundary. Running Sky allows the defense to attack the run without forfeiting pass distributions.

--

Putting the speed (two receivers) into the boundary changes everything. Unlike its sister formation where the running strength is to the boundary along with the back (three into), the two-speed FIB stresses the defense by putting an extra gap to the field. The stress comes from the dilemma of how to protect the defense against the run to the field while protecting itself against pass to the boundary. The answer is an adjustment in alignment.

When the tight end is to the boundary, the defense must cover down to the speed in space to the field, so the linebackers shift, or "Cheat" to the two-speed side. When the speed is into the boundary, the linebackers still must shift to the field to cover the extra gap. If the offense is going to put its best players in tight confines, the defense must force the offense to play in that limited space. Offenses put the speed to the boundary to get the defense to rotate, or to run high-low and switch concepts. Running a "Squeeze" alignment (shown on the next page) puts the linebackers towards the running strength to protect the defense from outside zone to the field.

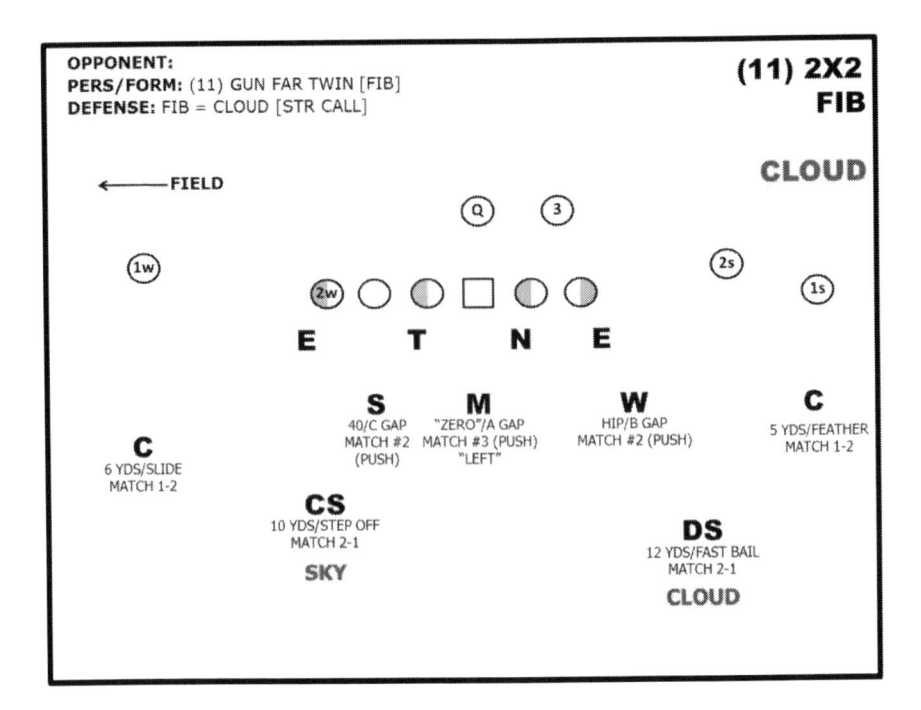

```
OPPONENT:                                              (11) 2X2
PERS/FORM: (11) GUN FAR TWIN [FIB]
DEFENSE: FIB = CLOUD [STR CALL]                            FIB

        ←——— FIELD                                       CLOUD

                              Q      3
      1w                                          2s
                     2w  ○  ◐  □  ◐  ○                    1s
                      E   T     N    E

                         S     M       W          C
                       40/C GAP "ZERO"/A GAP  HIP/B GAP  5 YDS/FEATHER
             C         MATCH #2 MATCH #3 (PUSH) MATCH #2 (PUSH) MATCH 1-2
          6 YDS/SLIDE  (PUSH)   "LEFT"
          MATCH 1-2
                             CS
                        10 YDS/STEP OFF          DS
                          MATCH 2-1         12 YDS/FAST BAIL
                             SKY               MATCH 2-1
                                                CLOUD
```

Running Cloud to the boundary allows the Will to be in less conflict and hang in his position. If the offense decides to RPO, there is a natural gap exchange by the defensive end and the Will that allows the Will to stay in a hipped position. The corner in Cloud is a quick trigger on any receiver screen, and the Will can be late from the box. The boundary safety is able to climb and sit on top of a condensed set to the boundary as well.

If the receivers run switch-verticals, the corner and safety will carry both and the Will can be late underneath, or push with a flaring back. In a pick/flat combination, the Will can push with the RB and the Mike is not aligned too far to cover the incoming sit route. Like in any quarters coverage, the corner and safety will vice (cone) the vertical, most likely a corner route by the #2 receiver.

The Sam and Mike are aligned far enough to the field that they will not get pinned on a stretch play. Running Sky to the field enables the CS to be quick to the "O" gap and carry the tight end if he goes vertical. The defensive end to the field should get hands on the tight end at the snap of the ball and hold his position, building a wall and creating a cutback. The "squeeze" alignment gives the defense an advantage by putting a quick force player to the boundary for screens and the linebackers to the field to combat stretch.

--

Trey Into

Trey is a unique set in its own right, and one of the hardest formations to defend in football. The added gap combined with a 3x1 set puts immense pressure on the defense. Like its sister in Trips, the defense should align in an Under Front. The only difference from 10 personnel is the defensive end to the tight end's side will align in a seven technique (or 6i - inside shade of the tight end). This helps to slow the tight end's release. The field side of Trey will look similar to its 10 personnel sister. The corner plays off man, but the difference is the field safety, which is playing Solo coverage. Solo allows the Mike to fit in his gap and hang in the low hole. The field safety will take the vertical of the tight end and "rob" the intermediate to the field if the tight end blocks or runs and underneath route. If a defensive coordinator is not comfortable with leaving the corner by himself with late intermediate help, he can lock the Mike on the tight end (man-to-man). Sam is aligned in a 10 to combat the run to the field. Like Trips, setting the three technique to the field builds a natural wall and creates a cutback. See below.

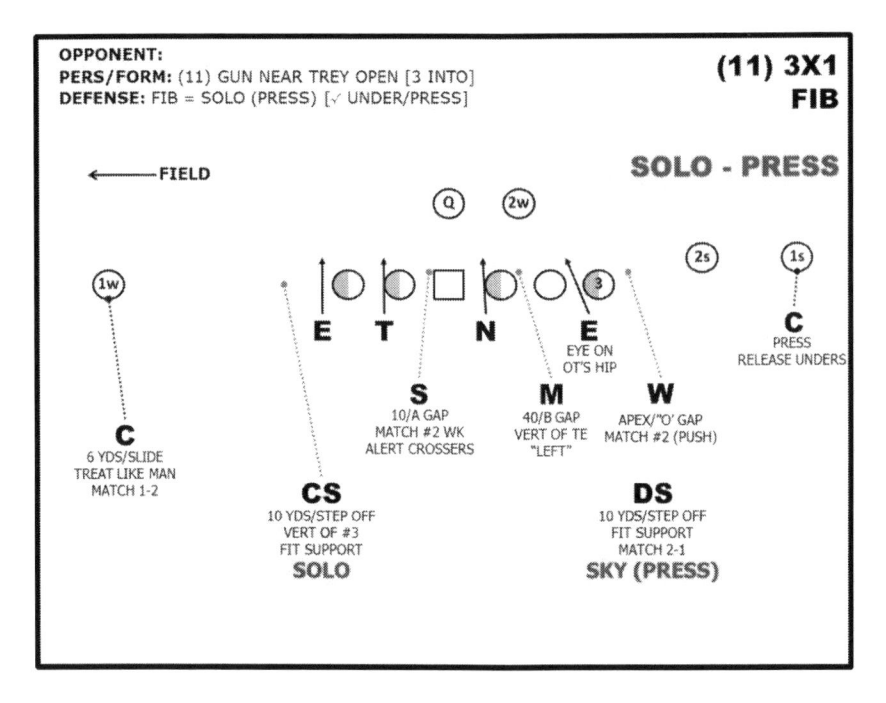

```
OPPONENT:
PERS/FORM: (11) GUN NEAR TREY OPEN [3 INTO]              (11) 3X1
DEFENSE: FIB = SOLO (PRESS) [√ UNDER/PRESS]                  FIB

←—— FIELD                                        SOLO - PRESS

                                                    E
                                                 EYE ON
                                                 OT'S HIP
                                                              C
                                                           PRESS
                                                     RELEASE UNDERS
  C                         S            M         W
6 YDS/SLIDE              10/A GAP     40/B GAP   APEX/"0" GAP
TREAT LIKE MAN         MATCH #2 WK   VERT OF TE  MATCH #2 (PUSH)
  MATCH 1-2           ALERT CROSSERS   "LEFT"

                         CS                         DS
                    10 YDS/STEP OFF            10 YDS/STEP OFF
                     VERT OF #3                  FIT SUPPORT
                     FIT SUPPORT                  MATCH 2-1
                        SOLO                    SKY (PRESS)
```

To the boundary, the Will aligns in an apex position and sets the edge. Mike is in a 40 to give him a plus alignment to combat speed option into the boundary. The corner to the Trey side is allowed to press and eliminate the #1 receiver and put an instant force player on any receiver screen. Pressing the corner also forces the offense into a low percentage throw (most likely a fade). With the reduced spacing, forcing the offense to run a fade route is a win for the defense, especially into the boundary where a safety will be able to help.

The boundary safety plays the two receivers just as if it were press quarters. An out route by #2 will trigger the boundary safety and the Will can break on ball thrown. Though a soft flat is a weakness in quarters, the reduced spacing forces the ball to be out quick with limited room for the receiver to turn op field. At the end of the day, Trey is a running set, but if teams do attack the defense through the air in FIB because the defense is running Solo, the boundary safety can switch to Cloud at any time, especially if the receivers stack or get too close to run Sky.

--

20 Personnel

Teams run 20 personnel formations into the boundary primarily to attack the defense through motion, mainly jet motion. If a defense has a tendency to spin to the two-speed side, the offense may opt to put the receivers into the boundary to create an advantage to the field. The best coverage to run into the boundary versus two-speed is Cloud because of the limited space, and the route combinations most offenses run (rub and switch routes). To the field, the coverage is Sky to create a hybrid man concept with the corner and to allow the field safety to "rob" the intermediate and hold the edge of the field versus run.

In the box, the Sam is in a 30 to combat any run to the field, and the Mike is in a 20 to give him a two-way go. It is important to note, the Mike is not double gapped, but FIB sets change the structure of the defense, and creates situations where rules have to be bent. In the case of 20 personnel, the Mike has to fit the "B" gap, but must also be able to run down a stretch to the field. The offense can run a QB stretch or jet motion with the slot back to the field.

If teams choose to run a high percentage of FIB out of 20, it is in the best interest of the defense to set the three technique to the field. The wall created by the three technique allows the Sam to be a free player if the offense attempts a jet sweep and holds the defensive end from chasing a down block.

Teams get into 20 personnel and put the speed to the boundary to try to run quick motions, or get the defense to spin to the two-speed side. To combat this, the defense needs to stay in a two-high shell and adjust to the speed motions with its linebackers. In the diagram below, the linebackers bump along with the motion. The Sam has the luxury of walking down towards the line. When the ball is snapped, technically the formation is a 30 personnel (three back) set. This allows the field safety to walk down to eight yards and play the intermediate "robber" technique afforded to him versus single receiver FIB sets and Sky coverage. The diagram shows the fits of each player outside of the box, essentially building a wall to create a cutback for the Mike and Will (do not forget the boundary safety too).

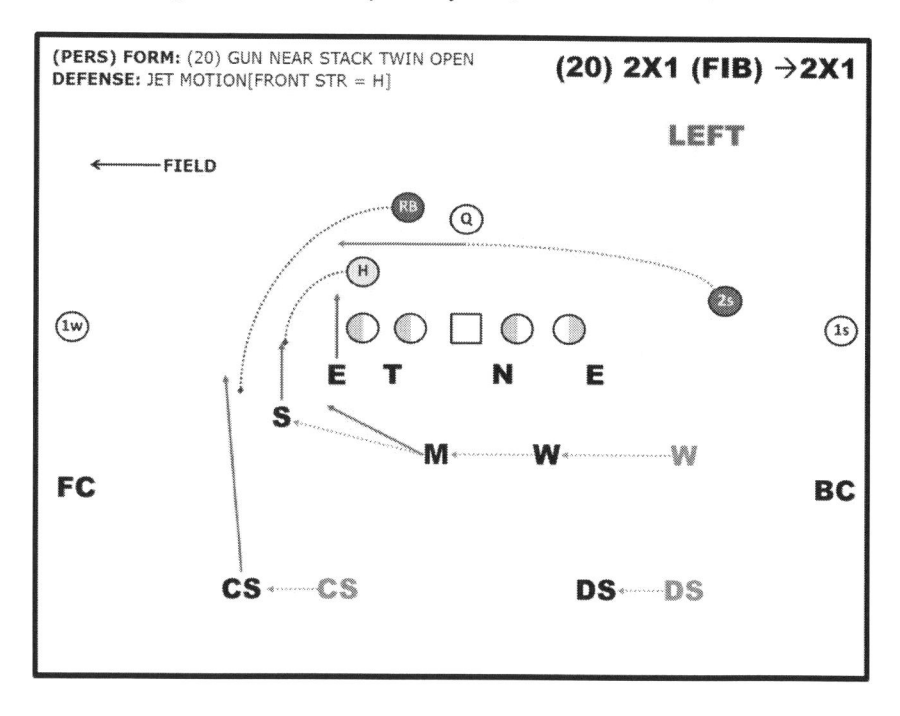

Conclusion

In order to combat FIB formations, the defense has to stay even and understand how the structure of the defense changes when the field of play is reduced. Setting the strength the correct way, and aligning correctly to spread formations will force the offense out of their FIB game plan. Many times, offenses use FIB to take advantage of a defensive tendency.

In order to reduce those tendencies the defense needs to stay as even as possible. A two-high scheme allows the defense to adjust with their linebackers and creates leverage on both sides of the formation. The one main issue, as in any defensive scheme, is when the offense runs a FIB to isolate the corner to the field. To combat this, the corner can play off man. Running Sky away from the FIB allows the field safety to sit in the intermediate zone and force low percentage throws or routes that are running into the defense's structure.

Defending Motion

"The greatest victory is that which requires no battle."

– Sun Tzu, *Art of War*

--

When defending teams that motion and shift, it is important for a defensive coordinator to understand one simple rule: if the defense does not move, the offense will stop moving. The key to defending motion is in the structure of a defense. The less a defense has to adjust to motion, the less the offense will use motion and shifts.

--

Offenses motion and shift to out leverage the defense, or to attack how a defense sets its strength (front). Auburn under Gus Malzahn, for example, has built an entire offense using wide receiver motions to move defenses into compromising positions or to out leverage the defensive alignment. Jet and other quick motions are a great way to get the defense moving in one direction.

Defenses are forced to move with the quick motions in order to gain outside leverage. When defenses rotate to match quick motions, the offense will attack the leverage with counter plays and play-action passes. This simple motion has allowed Auburn, and teams that run variations of the Slot-T, to expose defenses that over rotate, or try to spin to the motion.

Pro-style teams use the trading and shifting of offensive players to get the defense confused or over rotated (think Boise State under Harsin and Chris Petersen at Washington). In a pro-style offense, the tight end creates an extra gap and is used to take advantage of how the defense sets its strength. Offensive coaches like Brad Harsin at Boise St., previously Arkansas St. and Texas, have made a living on moving players around to gain an advantage on opponents.

Unlike the Auburn Slot-T jet motions that use speed to out leverage the defense, pro-style offensive shifts and motions use the defense's alignment and front rules to get a defense to align a certain way, then shift or motion to gain leverage. A benefit to all the movement is when teams run unbalanced sets, which is another way to out leverage the defense.

Motioning and shifting by the offense is a cat and mouse game. The offense moves its pieces around trying to find the weak spot in a defense. The key for the defense is to be sound and to move as little as possible. If the defense does not need to move, then the offense is just shifting to shift. A two-high scheme allows the defense minimal movement against teams that use motion and shifts by utilizing the linebackers.

Motion is the offense's way to isolate a player in man coverage or force the rotation of a defense. Defenses that are man heavy, and "lock" players on their man are attacked using motion. Offenses will motion a receiver to see if the defense is in man coverage, or to create a mismatch for the receiver going in motion.

Football is all about angles; motions and shifts give the offense a way to quickly reset the front and attack the defense. Tight end trades and multiple shifts force the defense to align the correct way and keep constant eye-discipline; much like the Swinging Gate during a PAT attempts forces the defense to account for every player. Eliminating the threat of motions and shifts really boils down to the way a defense sets its strength.

--

Defenses that have "strong" and "weak" sides are susceptible to shifts and motions because if an offense flips its formation, the defense must then realign as well. This can create a mass of humanity in the middle as defensive lineman and linebackers, even the safeties, are shifting from one side of the formation to the other. Much like spread tempo teams, teams that heavily shift understand that the defense wants to have certain players aligned to certain sides of a formation. By shifting or motioning, the offense is putting the defense on its heels, or forcing the defense to play "left-handed."

Once defenses realized that teams could hurt them by shifting, many began playing their defensive ends by field and boundary or left and right. Choosing to flip the interior lineman or shifting them over (minimal movement). Aligning this way eliminated the need to shift. A Nose and three technique trading places or shifting form one side of the guard to another is much simpler than two defensive ends, or the entire line, flipping sides as the ball is snapped. With the issue of swapping lineman solved, the linebackers were still in flux if the defensive coordinator is not aligning the linebackers by field (Sam) and boundary (Will).

In a 4-3, and even a 3-4, the linebackers were originally named for where they would line up. Sam goes to the strength, Mike stays in the middle, and the Will aligns himself on the weak side of the defensive strength call. Traditionally, most defenses aligned the Sam to the offense's strength, which usually was the tight end.

The next step in the evolution of offense was the shift to 11 personnel (more speed on the field). This caused problems for teams that set the strength to the tight end because the Will was now stuck guarding a receiver.

The shift to more athletic offensive sets forced defensive coordinators to change how they set the strength. As the pro-style spread (11/20 personnel) became more prevalent, the Sam linebacker became even more of a hybrid player, and defenses began to send him to the passing strength and away from the tight end. The Will became a pseudo-hybrid too, but more of a Mike who must be able to play in space. Once offenses figured out that the defense was setting the Sam to the passing strength, they began to put formations into the boundary (FIB) and run change of strength motions. By doing this, the defense was left with a Sam and Will flipped, and the offense at an advantage.

--

The next step in defending against the spread and its motions was to eliminate the Sam linebacker position altogether and replace him with an actual safety. In a basic 4-2-5 scheme, there are two strong safeties and one centerfield safety. The centerfield safety, or free safety, is never relied on to sink into the box. From the use of two "strong" safeties the *rock-and-roll* (or RnR) concept was born. The Mike and Will became box only defenders and rarely were asked to cover receivers.

In an RnR concept, there is a Spur (strong) and a Whip (weak) safety. The Spur is akin to the hybrid Nickels seen in defenses today, and the Whip is the Down Safety aligned to the boundary in most 4-2-5 quarters teams. When offenses shifted and motioned, the safeties would rotate, or *rock-and-roll* to reshuffle the secondary strength. Offenses soon took advantage and attacked the safety trying to backpedal into position.

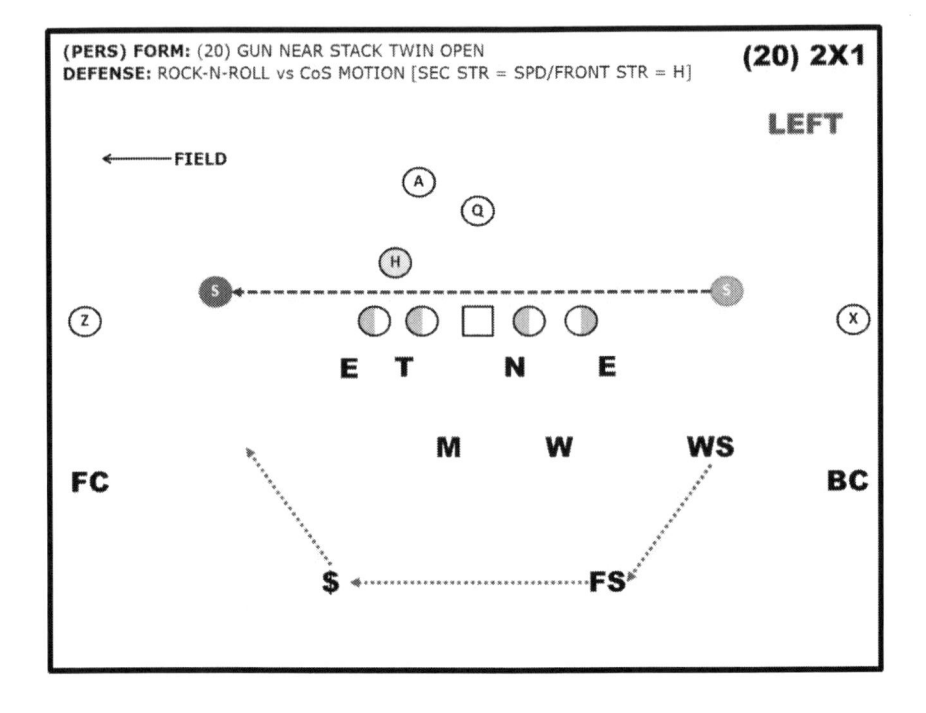

```
(PERS) FORM: (20) GUN NEAR STACK TWIN OPEN              (20) 2X1
DEFENSE: ROCK-N-ROLL vs CoS MOTION [SEC STR = SPD/FRONT STR = H]
                                                         LEFT
        ←—FIELD
                        A
                           Q
                        H
         S ←-------------------------------→ S
    Z                                              X
              E   T     N    E

              M    W    WS
    FC                                         BC

              $ ←·················· FS
```

--

This brings the journey full circle. In the beginning, defensive coordinators wanted to align their players by strong and weak to the tight end, but as offenses started to use shifts, they turned to setting the strength by field and boundary. This same cycle happened again as teams started to spread defenses out using spread formations. Defenses began defending the spread by aligning the Sam to the passing strength, but became exposed when teams used change-of-strength motion to put the Will and Sam in opposite roles. Again, defensive coordinators began shifting back to field/boundary calls.

--

Setting Up For Success

Spread offenses utilize two types of motion, quick and leveraging. Teams use the quick motions to get defenses to rotate or attempt to beat the defense to the edge. Leveraging motion is used when teams changing the strength to get the best match up or out leverage man coverage. To combat this, defenses need to have rules so players can line up quickly and absorb any motions they may see. An easy way to do this is by divorcing the front from the back seven.

With spread and the tempo style offense becoming the new norm for defensive coaches, the easiest way to align the strength, and put the defense in a "best case scenario" is to split the defense in half. In a split field quarters scheme, the Sam and Cover Safety go to the field. The Will and Down Safety will travel to the boundary. This alignment rule is based on the fact that most of the game of football is played on a hash.

Most offenses will not run their entire offense into the boundary (FIB) and if they do, the defense has done their job by making them left-handed and forced to play in limited space. With the introduction of hybrid players, and more and more defenses shrinking in size to gain speed to combat the spread, it is not too much to ask a hybrid Sam to fit into the box occasionally.

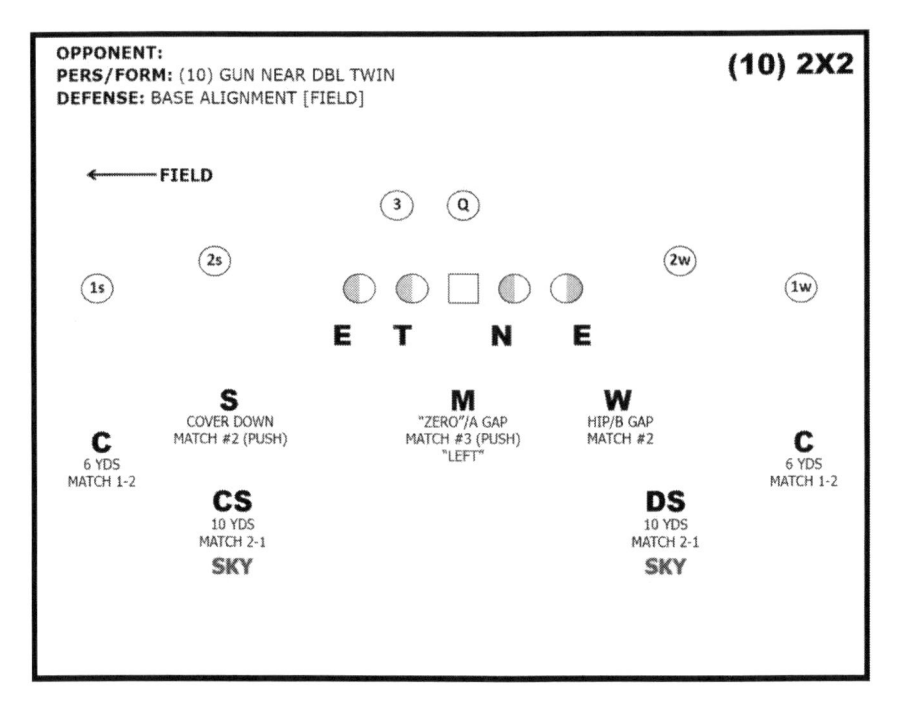

```
OPPONENT:
PERS/FORM: (10) GUN NEAR DBL TWIN                           (10) 2X2
DEFENSE: BASE ALIGNMENT [FIELD]

←——FIELD
                        3    Q
            2s                              2w
  1s                                                 1w
            E    T    N    E

            S              M              W
         COVER DOWN    "ZERO"/A GAP    HIP/B GAP
         MATCH #2 (PUSH)  MATCH #3 (PUSH)  MATCH #2
  C                     "LEFT"                      C
 6 YDS                                             6 YDS
MATCH 1-2     CS              DS                  MATCH 1-2
            10 YDS          10 YDS
            MATCH 2-1       MATCH 2-1
             SKY             SKY
```

In the diagram above, the strength is set to the field. If the ball is aligned in the middle of the field (MOF) the Sam will go to the same side as the back. Against spread teams, most quarters defenses will set the front to the field as well. Setting the three technique, or the front, to the field allows the Sam to gain a full cover down on the slot.

To the boundary, the Will is the fold player or conflict player. If the back jogs, or flips sides, nothing changes. The Will is still the fold/conflict player, and the Sam stays in a full cover down. By traveling players together, the defensive players will be able to self-correct, while also building comradery. The field safety (Cover Safety) and Sam will always travel to the field; the boundary safety (Down Safety) and Will are always going to align to the boundary. This alleviates the stress of waiting for the offense to line up. Against tempo spread teams, this split second gained can be the difference between an explosive play for the offense or a tackle for loss for the defense.

Divorcing the front from the strength call allows the defense to align quicker. The strength call only needs to be called once, to the front. The linebackers and the secondary know where to line up by the position of the ball on the field (hash or MOF). Creating a set of front rules and aligning by formation allows the defense to create quick anchor points for the defensive players to align. Alignments are quick and crisp. All dictated once the offense is set. If the offense puts the formation into the boundary (FIB), the defense will align how it normally would, except the Will and the boundary safety are now the traditional "strong" players.

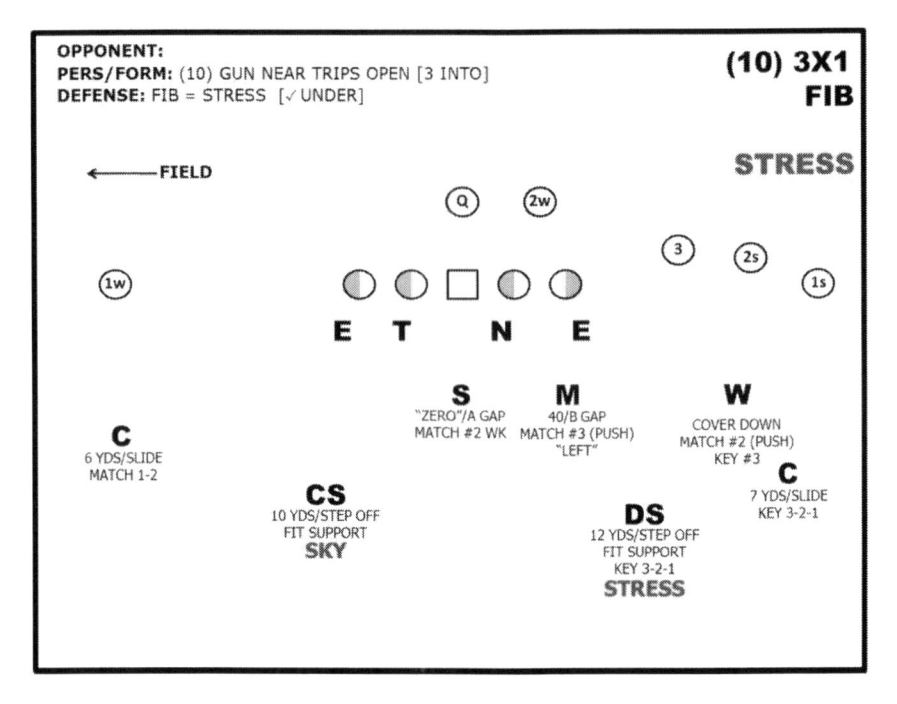

```
OPPONENT:                                                    (10) 3X1
PERS/FORM: (10) GUN NEAR TRIPS OPEN [3 INTO]
DEFENSE: FIB = STRESS [✓ UNDER]                                  FIB

        ←——— FIELD                                          STRESS

                        Q      2w
                                              3    2s
   1w         ○  ○  □  ○  ○                             1s
              E  T  N  E
                        S      M      W
                    "ZERO"/A GAP  40/B GAP   COVER DOWN
                    MATCH #2 WK  MATCH #3 (PUSH)  MATCH #2 (PUSH)
     C                            "LEFT"     KEY #3
  6 YDS/SLIDE                                       C
   MATCH 1-2        CS                          7 YDS/SLIDE
              10 YDS/STEP OFF        DS          KEY 3-2-1
               FIT SUPPORT      12 YDS/STEP OFF
                  SKY            FIT SUPPORT
                                  KEY 3-2-1
                                   STRESS
```

In the image to the above, the offense is aligned in a Trips formation and has put the formation into the boundary. The front is aligned in an Under Front (the rule for 3x1) and the Will covers down to the #2 receiver just like Sam would to the field. As more defenses turn to hybrid players, this concept is not difficult. The Mike never has to change. If the offense motions back to the field (change of strength motion) to create a 2x2 set, the linebackers adjust by "pulling the chain" and no one really moves. Sam still covers down to the #2 receiver, now to the field, and the Mike aligns in a "zero." The safeties do not go far either, coverages are adjusted and the defense is aligned correctly. Versus 10 personnel if the defense sets the front strength to the field it almost ensures, no matter what the offense does, that the front will not have to be reset. Even if the offense motions to 3x1 FIB, the front is aligned in an Under because it is set to the field.

--

Blitz Adjustments

The rules a defense creates to set its strength will directly correlate with how an offense chooses to attack it. As stated, offenses use motion as a leveraging tool. Setting the front and the Sam/Cover Safety duo to the field creates little movement when coming up against a motion/shift team. Even while blitzing, splitting the defense field/boundary and setting the front by formation can alleviate a multitude of issues. If a defense is a zone blitz team and blitzes by formation, the adjustments to movement should already be built into their base rules. The main issues with blitzing against motion teams are when an offense changes the strength.

Man blitzing gives the defense the luxury of having a two-shell look and does not give away the blitz because one safety is spinning. Against motion, being able to stay with a two-high shell allows the defense to move even less because no one is sinking back or coming down to meet the motion man. Players literally just slide or "plus" their alignments and are in position. Creating a blitz package with little adjustments to motion allows the defense to stay in the blitz rather than "Omaha," which is another reason why offenses use motion against blitzing defenses. Using man principles when blitzing allows the defense to send extra men to combat the offense's pass protection as well.

--

Top Motion Adjustments

The hardest motions to deal with are "change of strength" motions because it makes the whole defense adjust. Having a divorced front and setting the Sam and Cover Safety to the field allows for quick adjustments. Other than the linebackers and safeties adjusting to the width of the receivers, the interior linemen are the only ones that have to move, and if the front is set to the field may not happen at all.

A defense's base alignments should be able to align to anything at any time, even with motions and shifts. A tight end trade should only make the linebackers and interior lineman adjust. The way to combat motion is by not moving very far. If the defense does not need to flip or reshuffle everyone on the field, then offenses will just line up and play, making it easier for the defense.

--

On the following pages, view diagrams of the top three motion adjustments seen in today's game. With spread being the dominant form of football, it is not hard to fathom these three motions as being the top three seen by most defenses.

1. (10p) 2x2 to 3x1 change of strength motion:

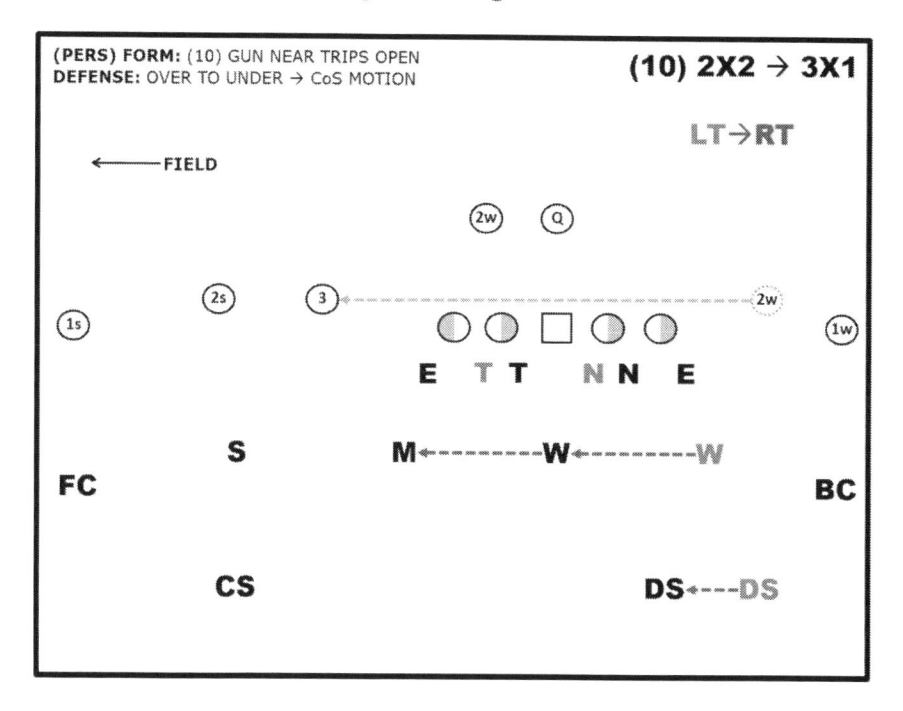

```
(PERS) FORM: (10) GUN NEAR TRIPS OPEN          (10) 2X2 → 3X1
DEFENSE: OVER TO UNDER → CoS MOTION
                                                   LT→RT
    ←——FIELD
                              2w    Q

              2s      3                              2w
    1s                   ○  ○  □  ○  ○              1w
                         E  T  T  N  N  E

              S           M←------W←--------W
    FC                                              BC

              CS                         DS←----DS
```

- 145 -

2. (20p) Across field motion (COS):

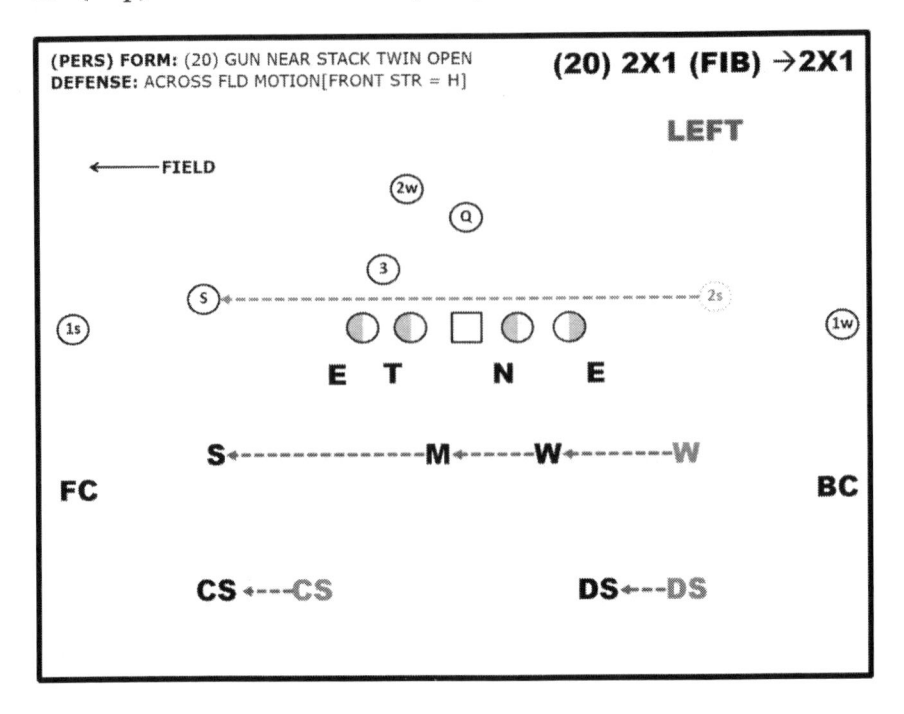

(PERS) FORM: (20) GUN NEAR STACK TWIN OPEN
DEFENSE: ACROSS FLD MOTION [FRONT STR = H]

(20) 2X1 (FIB) →2X1

LEFT

3. (10p) 2x2 to 3x1 change of strength motion:

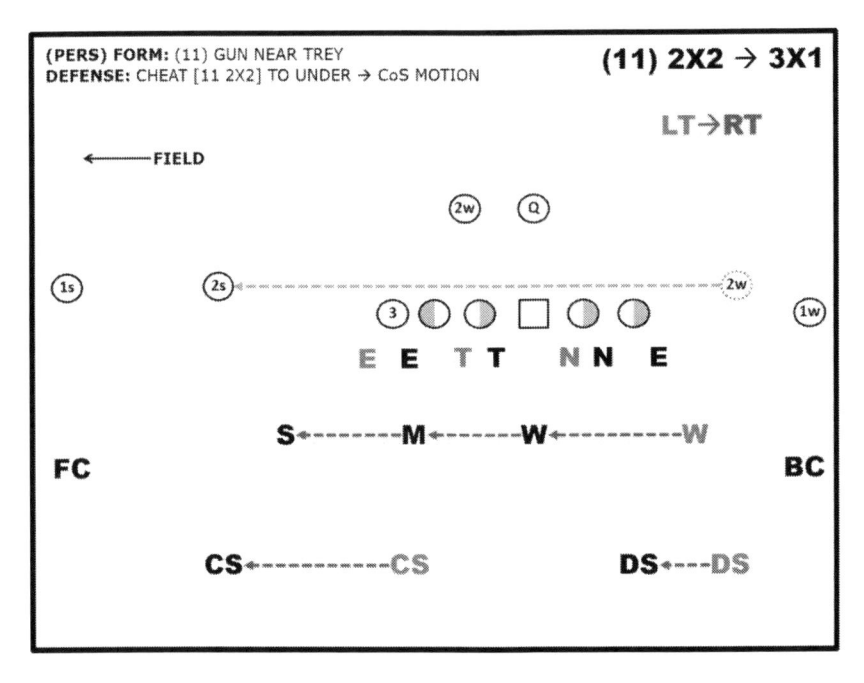

(PERS) FORM: (11) GUN NEAR TREY
DEFENSE: CHEAT [11 2X2] TO UNDER → CoS MOTION

(11) 2X2 → 3X1

LT→RT

Concerns/Conclusion

The main concern facing teams that set the Sam and Cover Safety to the field is what to do when teams go 3x1 into the boundary. In any 3x1 FIB, the Sam becomes the Mike. Even in 20 personnel, if a team chooses to set the formation into the boundary, the Sam becomes a box player. As defenses use more hybrid players to combat spread schemes, the concern for putting a smaller player in the box is real. Most offenses will not run their entire offense from inside the boundary, and if they do, the defense has done their job by forcing the offense to do what is not normal. If a defense must use the Sam is in the box, it can handle several plays a game where the Sam actually has to be the Mike.

Tempo and spread schemes force a defense to simplify. The best way to hold defensive formational integrity is to stay in a two-high shell and bump the linebackers on motion ("pull the chain"). Spread teams are concerned with width; they want to get their athletes in space. The main way to combat that is to put the defense's best athletes to the field. Divorcing the front strength from the back seven allows for flexibility and adaptiveness to any formation.

Here are some base rules to remember when defending motion:

1. Set the Sam and Cover Safety to the field, and set the strength of the defense to the field versus 10 personnel 2x2.
2. Keep the strength rules as simple as possible (Sam/Cover Safety to the field, strength to the field if 2x2 or to the tight end, and check Under to all 3x1 sets).
3. Do not be concern if the Sam is the Mike versus 3x1 FIB. If the offense wants to put all its athletes in limited space, it is making itself left-handed.
4. Use a "pull-the-chain" technique with the linebackers. With motion, even in man, all the linebackers have to do is adjust their alignments back to the base of the new formation.
5. If the defense does not move, flip, or reshuffle with motion, the offense will stop motioning.

Conclusion

--

For defensive coordinators who not only defend against the spread but coach alongside spread offenses, their defenses can play over two traditional games any given week. When Phil Bennett was hired in 2011 to be Baylor's defensive coordinator, he was asked to shore up a defense that was downright atrocious. Within two years he had created a defense that could come out of the shadows of the juggernaut offenses Art Briles had created.

Since 2012 (and until 2015) Baylor's defenses have ranked in the **top 50 in points per drive (PPD)**, even finishing 22nd in their first Big 12 Championship campaign in 2013. Combine those numbers with Baylor's seemingly unstoppable offense, and you have a winning recipe (50 wins in 5 years and two Big 12 championships). The turnaround was predicated on a set of rules to defend against the Big 12's arsenal of lethal spread teams. On the following page is the recipe.

--

Five Principles for Defending the Spread

--

1. **Have a plan for both the middle of the field and hash.** Offenses react differently when on the hash. Spread teams rely on quick, accurate throws, naturally many like to attack the boundary. How a defense plays the boundary is completely different than how it plays the field. Offenses are no different. The splits of the receivers are important too. Teams like Baylor under Art Briles, spread the defense to the max, where some teams use cluster sets to stress the coverage. When WRs line up tight to each other it is to the defense's advantage to play Cloud because the averages say the offense will run a high-low scheme or switch verticals. That being said, it does not make sense to run a Cloud scheme if the safety cannot reach the #1 receiver. Thus the conundrum that is the Briles Baylor offense. The receivers are not only wide, by they are clustered together. If the receiver's splits are too wide, or it is a run down, the defense should be in Sky. Running quarters allows the safeties to be aggressive in the run, or bracket the slot in the pass (helping your weakest pass defenders). By splitting the field a defense can react to exactly what the offense

gives them, switching from a Sky to Cloud seamlessly (...and never, in any circumstance, spin in the middle of the field).

--

2. **Play with the numbers in the box.** Most offensive coordinators only concern themselves with the front seven and who is physically located within the tackles. One way a defense can add numbers to the box is by using its safeties in the run fits. Running a match quarters scheme can give a defense up to nine players in the box. Along with run fits, a defense can manipulate the physical numbers within the box. By changing the number of players in the box, a defensive coordinator can create doubt, and doubt against tempo teams slows them down and creates turnovers. Hesitation = Turnovers. Turnovers = Wins.

--

3. **Add numbers to the box post-snap.** Adding numbers to the box post-snap challenges RPO teams. By adding numbers to the box after the snap, a defensive coordinator puts pressure on the run scheme, and hesitation on the reads by the QB. This can be done several ways; edge pressure, linebacker blitzes, or dropping a man from the secondary into the box. Spinning a safety down allows an outside linebacker to fold quickly into the box. Creating added numbers post-snap can change the reads for the QB and

give the defense an advantage. Many defensive coordinators want their defenses to move after the indicator (or snap signal). This may work for a while, but check-with-me teams will be able to "freeze" and adjust to the movement. Moving players post-snap allows the defense to stay static longer and create more hesitation as parts move when bullets are firing.

--

4. **Create doubts for the offense where the "B" gap is located.** Post-snap movement is one of the hardest things an offense faces, especially when it comes after the snap of the ball. **Changing the gaps post-snap** changes the read of the QB and puts pressure on zone teams. As offenses adjust during the game, a good offensive coordinator will be able to tell if the defense is exchanging gaps against their zone or playing straight-up gaps. Movements and pressures do not have to be exotic. An interior line stunt alone can muddy an RPO read because it changes the option responsibilities of the front seven. Depending on the movement, it can change the read completely. With moving pieces and gap exchanges, a good defensive coordinator can keep a spread offense on its heels and guessing.

--

5. **Always protect the vertical threat.** It is a pessimistic way of viewing defense, but in a match quarters scheme, a defensive coach has to assume that every play will end up being four verticals. Since the play "four verts" is the hardest play to defend in football, it makes sense for a defense to always retain the coverage piece to defend the "all go". Many defenses in the college ranks will not spin to single-high versus spread teams. This is by design because spinning creates too many one-on-one matchups and exposes the defense to high percentage throws. A defense should eliminate the most explosive play, keep everything in front of it, and create turnovers with pressures and line movements.

Cody Alexander

Thank You

--

The original template for the images that you see in this book were created by Casey Horny, current Special Teams Quality Control at the University of Texas. Casey is an extraordinary defensive mind and has an unmatched desire to win. Casey and I worked closely during my time at Baylor. He helped me develop the hit charts, play templates, and breakdowns you see in this book and on the website, MatchQuarters.com.

After Bennett and my father, Casey is probably the next most influential person on my coaching philosophy. Where Jim Gush was my emotional rock while at Baylor, Casey was the compass for my attention to detail, always demanding excellence. Between Bennett and Casey no stone was left unturned. It would be a disservice if I did not express my gratitude for the three years Casey and I worked together.

As stated above and in the prologue, Jim Gush was my emotional rock during my time at Baylor and I am still close with him today. He made it possible to work under that extreme pressure. Needless to say, there were many times I hung my head and wanted to quit (many GAs find themselves there), but Gush always picked me back up. His belief in me sprung me back to life. For that, I am grateful.

--

Lastly, this book would not have been possible without so many people who I have met through my website and coaching career. Every day I am pushed to explain my stance on football and develop my schemes. To my followers on Twitter and those that are regulars to the MatchQuarters.com site, thank you. Without your support this book would not be possible.

--

Below is a list of those who were a critical part to what went into this book and have helped me become the coach I am today. To them I say thank you (no particular order):

--

Jon and Melanie Pope

Coach Art Briles

... and the rest of the Baylor Football staff from 2011-2014

Tim Denton (unofficial editor of MQ & created the cover photo)

Beth Lowry, Kent Messer, Yazz Topchick,

and the rest of the staff at Willow Springs Middle School

Ryan Cox and the 2015 Lovejoy Football staff (3 to 9!)

Ian Boyd

Alex Kirby

Chris B. Brown

Rick Butler

Dr. James Petersen

Sheryl Honeycutt and the rest of THSCA

...and to all my boys at Lovejoy:

Beau, Bump, Chase, Landon,

Luke, Jake C., Jake I., & Pfaff.

You will always be my favorite crew!

--

A very special thank you must go to my wife, Jillian.

Her strength inspires me every day.

Cody Alexander

I want to end this book the way I always do at MatchQuarters.com:

--

As always, support the site by following me on Twitter (*@The_Coach_A*) and spreading the word to your coaching friends by liking and retweeting the articles you read (*even sharing them via Facebook and LinkedIn*).

Do not hesitate to email me with questions through the site's CONTACT page or through my DM on Twitter. I enjoy speaking with you guys (*iron sharpens iron*).

– Coach A.

--

MatchQuarters.com

MQx

#ArtofX

© 2017 MatchQuarters.com | Cody Alexander

Made in the USA
Lexington, KY
06 December 2018